University
Students and
Revolution
in Cuba,
1920-1968

University
Students and
Revolution
in Cuba,
1920-1968

By Jaime Suchlicki

Ⓜ

**UNIVERSITY OF
MIAMI PRESS**
Coral Gables, Florida

Contents

Foreword

Student political activity has a long history in Latin America, and students have initiated successful movements in many countries. Cuban students have participated in political activity for a century or more, but organized student movements date only from the 1920's. Because of the insensitivity of the Machado and Batista regimes to the need for reforms, in the 1930's the students began employing violence to make their demands heard. Under the concept of university autonomy the police were excluded from the campus of the University of Havana, which thereupon became a sanctuary and base for terrorist groups that were only loosely allied with the students.

The use of violence or other illegal methods is a dangerous precedent for any group, however worthy it may consider its motives, even though it believes that nothing short of terrorism will force the government to heed its demands. But those who justified their own violence by the purity of their motives soon saw other groups employing the same methods for less lofty reasons. If students use terror and violence to bring about changes they seek, they cannot deny the same means to others. Violence, terrorism, and repression became characteristic of Cuban politics, and foreign conspirators offered a wide range of ideologies and formulas for solving all of Cuba's problems.

Dr. Suchlicki has made a perceptive study of student political activism in Cuba in the four decades before the Castro take-over, a study that will contribute much to our understanding of student unrest in Latin America and elsewhere as well as to an appreciation of the roots of the Cuban Revolution. Dr. Suchlicki indicates that there is little likelihood of serious student demonstrations as long as Fidel Castro maintains his suffocating grip on the universities. "Counterrevolutionaries" are denied admission, the makeup of the student body has changed, and emphasis is now on science and technology. But elsewhere in Latin America university autonomy survives, and the political activities of the University of Havana students are part of a continuing struggle that has recently appeared on various university campuses in the United States. Both student activists and university officials may find some profit, if not solace, in this analysis of student political activism in Cuba.

DONALD E. WORCESTER

Fort Worth, Texas
April, 1969

Preface

Latin American students have been traditionally active in politics. Student elites have been in the forefront of the struggles against dictatorship and of the drive for modernization. Leaders today of nearly every important political party were student leaders in their youth. Universities and the military are two of the main sources of leadership in Latin America. Universities are, furthermore, microcosms of their countries' political life, providing an ideal laboratory for the study of Latin American politics.

The attention given to Latin American students has increased in the past several years. The activism displayed by American students in the 1960's has further increased interest in student politics. Studies of the student movement of several countries have appeared. Yet, before valid generalizations can be made, there is need for in depth studies on the role of students in the various Latin American countries.

This book focuses primarily on a specific group of students, namely those at the University of Havana during the years 1920–1968. The importance of the University of Havana students is not based simply on the fact that they were, and continue to be, the largest university student body in Cuba. This group was chosen because of its historically important participation in Cuba's political development and especially because of its prominent role in the Cuban revolution.

It is my hope that this book can shed some light on two very fascinating subjects: the roots of the Cuban revolution and the changes that have taken place among students and in the universities since Castro came to power. It is impossible, I believe, to understand the Cuban revolution without an understanding of the history of Cuba's student movement. How did the students contribute to bring about the revolution? What was Fidel Castro's role as a student activist? What happens to a student movement in a post-insurgency phase? What changes have taken place at the once autonomous Cuban universities? How is Castro able to mobilize and control the students? Answers to these and other questions are attempted in the following pages.

I could fill several pages with the names of those to whom I owe a debt of gratitude. I am grateful to numerous Cubans for their eagerness to help and their patience with my incessant questioning.

I am indebted to the University of Miami's Center for Advanced International Studies and particularly to its Director, Mose L. Harvey, for allowing me time to complete the research for this study. The Center's stimulating atmosphere created, furthermore, the needed momentum to finish the book. I am also grateful to the Ford Foundation, whose grant to the Center for studies on Cuba supported my own research on the Cuban students.

I am especially indebted to Professor Donald E. Worcester. Studying under his direction at Texas Christian University was a challenging and rewarding experience. I am very grateful to him for writing the foreword to this book.

I am most grateful to Professors Ernst Halperin and Lowry Nelson for reading the manuscript and making valuable criticisms that helped clarify my own thoughts. Jay Mallin made valuable editorial suggestions, which I appreciate. For the book's errors and shortcomings I alone am, naturally, responsible. To my wife Carol I am deeply grateful. Her enduring patience made this book possible.

JAIME SUCHLICKI

May, 1969

1

Stirrings of
Cuban Nationalism

Organized student political activism did not begin in Cuba until the 1920's, but participation of Cuban students in politics goes back to the period of Cuba's struggle for independence in the early 1870's. During that time the few schools at the University of Havana, staffed almost entirely by *criollos* after its secularization in 1842, became the hothouses of anti-Spanish sentiment. In October, 1871, the island's governor, Conde de Valmaseda, complaining that "professors had escaped abroad to carry on activities against the government and that students were joining the rebellion against Spain," issued a decree forbidding the granting of several doctoral degrees at the University of Havana.[1] The Spanish government thereby attempted to reduce the University's importance and to punish the students for their rebelliousness.

A more dramatic event and one of long-lasting influence occurred that same year. On November 27, 1871, Spanish authorities tried and executed eight University of Havana medical students accused of having desecrated the grave of a Spanish officer and imprisoned thirty-four more students accused of anti-Spanish activities. Whether or not the students were involved in subversive actions is not known, but the government intended this punishment to serve as an example for other students and for the population in general. Instead of reducing opposition, the incident shocked Cuban society and further inflamed anti-Spanish sentiment at the University of Havana.[2] The students' martyrdom was memorialized by the students of following generations who continued to commemorate the events of 1871 not only as an example of Spanish cruelty, but also as a precedent in their struggle against tyranny and oppression.

It was the task of a young student, José Martí, to create a feeling of separatism among his compatriots and to lead his country toward a war of independence against Spain. Martí is Cuba's most famous hero and most influential writer. Imprisoned and exiled during his high school years, Martí realized very early that independence from Spain was the only solution for Cuba. He felt that no concession could be expected from Spain. Fearful of United States intervention in Cuban affairs, he advocated a fast and decisive war. Martí's pilgrimage throughout the Americas in the 1880's, at a time when the Cubans were leaderless and divided, helped to unite and organize them. For more than a decade, Martí's efforts were directed toward the realization of his dream: the independence of Cuba. So well had he organized the anti-Spanish forces that his order for the uprising early in 1895 assured the ultimate expulsion of Spain from the island. The war, however, was not the fast and decisive struggle he had sought. It took his own life early in 1895, dragged on for three more years, and eventually prompted the American intervention (1899–1902) that he had feared.

Martí believed that Cuba had to be liberated not only from Spain but from the legacy of Spanish social customs and vices. This would come slowly, as a process of political maturity and education that without hate would establish the foundation of a healthy republic. The new nation would be based on close collaboration of all social classes, and not on the struggle of one class against another. It would be the fatherland where everyone could live in peace, with freedom and justice—a nation based on law, order, and the hard work of its people.[3] Martí believed, furthermore, in each peasant owning his own plot of land, in a diversified economy less dependent on sugar, and in an economically independent nation.[4]

His vision of a socially harmonious and economically independent nation failed to materialize in the post-independence years. Whether Martí would have been able to prevent the events that followed the war of independence can only be conjectured. A process of centralization extended the great sugar estates of the colonial period, thus restraining the growth of a rural middle class and creating a landless agrarian peasantry. Cuba became more and more commercially dependent on the United States, and the inclusion of the Platt Amendment into the Cuban Constitution of 1901 established United States supervision of political developments in Cuba.[5]

Cuba's social system also preserved the colonial Spanish attitude that public office was a source for personal profit. Electoral frauds became a standard practice. Politics became the means to social advancement, a contest between factions for the spoils of office. *Personalismo** was substituted for principle, and allegiance to a man or a group the only way to insure survival in the political arena. Although the United States dissolution of Cuba's veteran army prevented a repetition of the typical nineteenth century Spanish-American experience, where the army filled the political vacuum left by Spain, many of the war veterans took an active part in politics, and their influence was felt in the years following the establishment of the Republic in 1902. [6]

By filling the vacuum left by Spain as the overseer of the island's affairs, the United States unwittingly perpetuated the Cubans' lack of responsibility. Cubans enjoyed the assurance that the United States would intervene to protect them from

* According to George I. Blanksten, "Political Groups in Latin America," *American Political Science Review,* vol. LIII, no. 1 (March, 1959), *personalismo* may be defined as "the tendency to follow or oppose a political leader on personality rather than ideological grounds, through personal, individual, and family motivations rather than because of an impersonal political idea or program."

foreign entanglements or to solve their domestic difficulties, as occurred in 1906. The situation only encouraged their irresponsible and indolent attitude toward their own affairs and was not conducive toward responsible self-government. In the early decades of the Republic, the Cubans found it easy to rely upon the United States for guidance in their political decisions. "Tutelage," wrote Cuban intellectual Jorge Mañach, "favored the growth of general civic indolence, a tepid indifference to national dangers." [7]

Disregard for educational matters served to aggravate an already precarious situation. Critics who argued for an educational system in accord with the country's needs were ignored.[8] The University of Havana, founded in 1728, was the only center of higher learning in Cuba.[9] During the first United States intervention (1899–1902), and under the leadership of Secretary of Public Instruction Enrique José Varona, a variety of reforms were introduced, more facultades were added, impetus was given to scientific and technical studies, tuition was reduced, and the campus was moved from the Santo Domingo Convent to its present location. Varona's reforms attracted new students, and in 1901 enrollment increased to 662 from the previous year's 381. The total University budget was also increased from $206,000 to $260,000 annually.[10]

Despite this relative progress, the University was far from fulfilling its important educational tasks. It lacked proper financial resources, a competent full-time faculty, and an up-to-date system of education. Law and medicine were the most popular professions—the first because of its importance as a stepping-stone for political prominence, and the second because of its associated social status. Although the Cuban countryside was in need of doctors, most of them remained in Havana, attracted by the existing opportunities and cosmopolitan atmosphere of the capital city.

Writing almost thirty years later, University of Havana professor Pablo F. Lavín complained about Cuba's educational backwardness, pointing out the numerous ills the country suffered. Among these were an excessive number of professional men, the poor facilities of the University, and the lack of professors. Professor Lavín also criticized the verbalistic and memorizing method of learning being employed at the University. "There exists," he explained, "a divorce between education and the social and economic needs of the country." [11]

The failure of Cuban society to absorb university graduates accentuated the feelings of frustration in a generation that found itself with little opportunity to apply its acquired knowledge. The severe economic crisis with its accompanying economic chaos and social misery that affected Cuba in 1920 accelerated the desire for change, leading to a questioning of the existing order of society.

Discontented groups attempted to induce morality and reforms into Cuba's public life. A group of intellectuals founded the "Cuban Council of Civic Renovation." In newspaper and magazine articles they criticized the corruption of President Alfredo Zayas' administration. Workers formed the Havana Federation of Workers and organized several strikes requesting better wages and working conditions. A number of war veterans sponsored a movement called the "Association of Veterans and Patriots" whose actions finally led in 1924 to a short-lived revolt against the government.[12]

THE UNIVERSITY REFORM
MOVEMENT OF 1923

The failure of these groups to achieve the needed reforms led to a generational conflict, and the University of Havana students assumed the role of leaders in the brewing revolution. Influenced by the reformist ideas emanating from the Córdoba Reform Movement and from the Mexican and Russian revolutions, the students began searching for answers to Cuba's problems. Close supervision of Cuban affairs by the United States became the objective of their attacks, for most of the island's difficulties were blamed on the northern neighbor. When the University of Havana Council, composed of faculty and administrative officials, considered offering United States Special Envoy Enoch H. Crowder an honorary degree, students rioted and demonstrated against the United States.[13]

University of Buenos Aires Rector José Arce's visit to the University of Havana late in 1922 increased student effervescence. Arce lectured at the campus on the accomplishments of the Córdoba Reform Movement and on the methods employed by the Argentinian students to obtain their demands. His words inspired his listeners and prompted the creation of the Directorio de la Federación de Estudiantes (Student Federation), the occupation of university buildings by the students, and the organization of short-lived student strikes.[14]

This reform movement was concerned with the university as an institution and with its cultural role in society. The students wanted a modern university in accord with Cuba's needs, administered with their participation, available to the less privileged sectors of society, and sheltered from government interference.[15] "We realized the failures of our educational system," explained Aureliano Sánchez Arango, a student activist of those days and later Minister of Education during President Carlos Prío's administration, "and we wanted a university that could fit the needs of our country." [16] The students obtained a series of academic and administrative reforms, larger government subsidies, and the establishment of a University Commission composed of professors, students, and alumni. The Commission drew plans to reform the university and purged several professors accused of "senility and incompetence." [17] The students were unsuccessful, however, in their demand for university autonomy. Perhaps aware that such a measure would create a sanctuary for political agitators, the government refused to grant the University's autonomy.

One of the principal leaders of the reform movement was Julio Antonio Mella, a young law student of strong anti-American feelings. Born out of wedlock in Havana in 1903,

Mella was raised by his father, a tailor of Dominican ancestry, after his British mother had moved to New Orleans. During his school days at the Newton Academy in Havana, Mella fell under the influence of one of his teachers, the exiled Mexican poet Salvador Díaz Mirón. Díaz Mirón's narratives of the Mexican Revolution inspired his young listener with ideas of social justice and political reform. After an unsuccessful trip to Mexico and New Orleans in 1920 to study for the military profession, Mella entered the University of Havana.[18]

A powerful speaker and a constant agitator, the handsome, dark complexioned, athletically built Mella became the idol of the University students. He participated in student demonstrations against President Alfredo Zayas and United States Envoy Enoch Crowder, and became Secretary General of the Student Federation. Mella spearheaded the university reform movement, organizing in 1923 the First Congress of Cuban Students. For him the university reform movement transcended the academic walls. Mella considered it part of a social struggle to better the conditions of the less privileged sectors of society, calling the movement "another battle of the class struggle." [19] Inspired by Víctor Raúl Haya de la Torre's "Popular University González Prada" in Lima, Mella founded in Havana the short-lived "Popular University José Martí," a leftist institution devoted to the education of the workers.[20] In addition to editing two magazines, *Alma Mater* and *Juventud,* Mella also organized the Anti-Imperialist League and the Anti-Clerical Federation.[21]

Through these activities Mella became associated with several Cuban Marxists. Carlos Baliño, a prestigious figure of Cuba's war of independence and later founder of the Communist Association of Havana, collaborated closely with Mella in *Juventud,* bringing the young student into the association. Encouraged by the Mexican Communist Party and supported by its envoy in Havana, Enrique Flores Magón, Baliño and Mella called a congress of all Communist groups in the island for August, 1925. The number of militant Communists in

Cuba was small, and of the nine Communist groups only four sent delegates.[22]

From this 1925 congress emerged the Cuban Communist Party. José Miguel Pérez, a Spanish Communist, was appointed Secretary General, and the party was soon affiliated with the Communist International. Mella became one of its most important leaders, entrusted to propagandize the creation of the party, to edit its newspaper, *Lucha de Clases,* and to direct the education of new party members.[23] Rolando Meruelo, a prominent party member, related that although the party was small and disorganized, the Communists soon formed a Youth League, using Mella and other student leaders to agitate and to gain followers within the University.[24]

By 1925 Mella and a small group of students directed their attacks against President-elect Gerardo Machado. At a time when the regime enjoyed much support, Mella sensed Machado's authoritarian nature and labeled him a "tropical Mussolini." [25] Mella's activities first clashed with University authorities, who expelled him temporarily, and then with Machado, who accused him of a terrorist act and jailed him. Mella went on a nineteen-day hunger strike. Finally, the pressure of public opinion forced Machado to release him. After fleeing to Mexico, Mella traveled to Belgium in 1927 and later on to the Soviet Union to attend Communist meetings. His turbulent life ended mysteriously in 1929 at the hands of a paid assassin in Mexico, shortly after breaking up with the Communists and being expelled from the Mexican Communist Party. Mella's death is still surrounded by mystery. Communists quickly blamed Machado. Mella's widow, Olivín Zaldívar, however, insisted that Mella was killed by assassins hired by Machado's agent, Jose Magriñat, who worked with Vittorio Vidali, alias Luis Sormenti or Carlos Contreras, a known Comintern agent. "Sormenti had warned Mella," stated Mrs. Zaldívar, "that he could leave the Communist International only either expelled or dead." [26]

It is indeed difficult to determine what motivated a student leader such as Mella. His paternal grandfather's prominent role in the Dominican Republic's independence movement may have inspired within him a desire to fight against oppression. His ancestry of mixed nationality enhanced his search for identity and for recognition. A society that scorned illegitimate birth made him feel like an outcast, increasing his bitterness and frustration. "Even his half-sisters rejected him," revealed Mella's widow, "refusing to have anything to do with their brother." [27] Mella embraced communism and found in it a reason for his existence. For him, communism offered an ideology that promised to bring justice to Cuba's economic and social system, creating order out of the existing chaos. But of more importance, it offered him a cause for which to fight and an escape valve for his tormented personality.

Mella can be considered only partially representative of his student generation. He shared with his University colleagues a desire to improve the educational and political conditions of Cuba and to oppose United States supervision of Cuban affairs. He differed from them, however, in that he renounced his generation's romantic nationalism and vague ideological conceptions to embrace an international movement devoted to the overthrow of the existing order and to the establishment of a proletarian dictatorship.

2

The Student
Generation of 1930

By 1927, the university reform movement of 1923, which had started as a crusade for academic reform, developed political overtones. Machado's decision to remain in power for another term was the spark that ignited student opposition. Claiming that his economic program could not be completed within his four-year term and that only he could carry it out, Machado announced his decision to reelect himself and to extend the presidential term to six years. Whereas similar attempts by earlier presidents had resulted in rebellion, Machado's decision only brought about a wave of national indignation against the invalidation of suffrage. The regime still enjoyed the support of large sectors of society. Increased revenues had brought prosperity, and Machado's improved administration, especially in the field of public works, had gained him a strong following. Machado, furthermore, prevented the growth of political opposition by winning control of the Conservative Party and aligning it with his own Liberal Party and also with the small Popular Party. Through bribes and fear Machado was able also to subordinate Congress to the Executive's will.

Machado's attempted reelection met with stern student opposition at the University of Havana. While the Cuban Senate debated a bill in June of 1927 legalizing the regime's permanence in power, students unsuccessfully attempted to penetrate the Senate chamber to protest the measure. They were met by police repression and several students were beaten and wounded.[2] Student disorders soon spread to other parts of the island. On June 19 and 20 a number of university students were arrested in Pinar del Río and Matanzas provinces while holding anti-Machado rallies.[3] Machado took immediate measures to prevent further demonstrations. He temporarily closed the University, dissolved the Student Federation, and abolished the University Commission.[4]

These measures, however, failed to control the students completely. A small but active group organized a Directorio Estudiantil Universitario (University Student Directorate) in mid-1927 to oppose the regime. "An organization was needed," explained Aureliano Sánchez Arango, one of the founders of the Directorio, "because we had no Student Federation and we met with considerable opposition within the student body itself, which was sympathetic toward the regime." [5] The Directorio issued a manifesto defending the right of university students to discuss politics and attacking Machado's reelection attempts. Students demonstrated in front of the University, shouting anti-Machado slogans and tearing down government posters. Machado rapidly retaliated. Following his orders, the University Council, composed of faculty and administrative officials, formed disciplinary tribunals and expelled most of the Directorio leaders from the University.[6]

The expulsion of the rebellious youths brought only temporary peace. Machado's unopposed reelection in November, 1928, provided new ammunition for student protests, while Mella's assassination in 1929 furnished the martyr whose memory spurred student hatred of Machado.[7] Throughout 1929 the expelled leaders of the 1927 Directorio renewed their contacts with university students. In September, 1930, they established a second Directorio, agreed to issue a manifesto condemning the regime, and planned a massive demonstration for September 30. [8]

The demonstration ended in disaster. When police attempted to break up the gathering, a riot developed and a policeman fatally wounded Directorio leader Rafael Trejo. Several other students and policemen were also wounded.[9] Trejo's death unloosed a wave of anti-Machado feeling. The government responded this time by closing the University and many high schools. The University of Havana remained closed until 1933. [10] Forbidden by the police to hold open meetings, the students developed what they called *tánganas* (impromptu gatherings of protest). The tánganas first led to clashes with the police and later to organized violence and terrorism.

STUDENTS AGAINST MACHADO: THE OPPOSITION TRIUMPHS

Trejo's death was the turning point in the struggle against the regime. After September, 1930, the Cubans viewed the courageous student generation that battled Machado's police with admiration and respect. For some, "the generation of 1930," as these students were later known in Cuban history, seemed irresponsible and undisciplined, while for others it became the best exponent of disinterested idealism. Embattled by the first shock waves of the world depression and oppressed by an increasingly ruthless dictator, many Cubans, especially among the less privileged sectors of society, turned in hope and despair toward these youngsters. They deposited their faith in a generation that, although inexperienced and immature, seemed incorruptible and willing to bring morality to Cuba's public life.

Student and government confrontation gained momentum with the closing of the University. Unable to attend classes, many students joined the anti-Machado ranks. As time passed the students became convinced that only armed action would force Machado to relinquish power. Urban violence, a hitherto almost unknown phenomenon in Cuba's political history, flourished.

The regime responded to each demonstration with harsher measures. But for every student beaten or arrested by police, new students emerged to pick up the banner of revolt. On January 3, 1931, police arrested twenty-two students—among them Directorio leaders Carlos Prío Socarrás, Aureliano Sánchez Arango, and Rubén de León—accusing them of plotting against the government.[11] On February 14, eighty-five University of Havana professors, almost the entire faculty, were indicted on charges of sedition and conspiracy to overthrow the regime. Among those arrested was Dr. Ramón Grau San Martín, a distinguished physiology professor. The professors were later released pending investigation, but Machado refused to release the rebellious youngsters.[12] Late in 1931, student leader Willy Barrientos conspired within the army to take over Camp Columbia and depose Machado. The government discovered the plot and arrested the principal conspirators. The *porra* (Machado's secret police) murdered two of the plotters. Barrientos escaped to the United States.[13]

While the principal leaders of the Directorio were in jail in 1931, a split developed and a small group formed a splinter organization, the Ala Izquierda Estudiantil (Student Left Wing). The reasons for the split were varied. First, the two groups differed in economic background. Zoila Mullet, Directorio activist and later Minister of Education during Batista's second administration, points out that "while most of the Ala Izquierda leaders came from poorer homes, those of the Directorio were primarily from middle class ones." [14] There was also a certain amount of jealousy between the two groups. Sánchez Arango, who became the Ala Izquierda leader, explained that some from his group resented the better treatment others received in jail.[15] Finally, there were ideological differences. Strongly influenced by Marxist ideas and more radical in their outlook, Ala Izquierda members opposed the relations Directorio leaders maintained with Cuba's political parties and politicians. "We wanted," emphasized Sánchez Arango, "a complete divorce from the past." [16] Many of the Ala Izquierda leaders embraced communism. Some, like Sánchez Arango, dissillusioned with the Communists, broke away from them after Machado's downfall.

During the anti-Machado insurrectionary period, the Ala Izquierda became merely a tool of the Cuban Communist Party. The party, led by Rubén Martínez Villena, a popular poet and intellectual, directed the organization's activities and used it to influence the student movement. Raúl Roa, one of its members (later Castro's Minister of Foreign Relations), explained that "the Ala, as well as the Anti-Imperialist League, were parallel organizations of the Cuban Communist Party." [17]

Throughout most of his regime, the Communists opposed Machado and advocated, as the only correct strategy to overthrow his government, the mobilization of the proletariat, culminating in a general strike.[18] They insisted that only the proletariat constituted a truly revolutionary class; its hegemony would guarantee the victory of all the oppressed classes and the ultimate social revolution, which would end all class conflicts.[19] The Caribbean Bureau of the Communist International urged the party in those days to cooperate with the anti-Machado forces with the specific objective of gaining leadership of the revolutionary movement. This did not mean, however, the creation of united fronts, but rather taking control of the anti-Machado movement by emphasizing the idea of class struggle and by appealing to the soldiers and workers to join the Communist cause. The Cuban Communists were ordered, furthermore, to split the anti-Machado movement by denouncing non-Communist leaders as "outs" who were only interested in power.[20] "The Cuban Communists," stressed Meruelo, suffered in those days from extremism and radicalism, another reason why they couldn't get along with anti-Machado leaders." [21]

The Directorio and the Ala Izquierda were not the only groups opposing Machado. The Unión Nacionalista, headed by a war of independence colonel, Carlos Mendieta, also condemned the regime in newspapers and in public demonstrations. In 1931 Mendieta and former President Mario G. Menocal organized a short-lived uprising in Pinar del Río Province. That same year, a group led by engineer Carlos Hevia and newspaperman Sergio Carbó equipped an expedition in the United States and landed in Oriente Province, only to be crushed by Machado's army. In New York, representatives of several anti-Machado organizations united and formed a revolutionary junta. Although the Directorio sent delegates to the New York meetings, the students did not formally join the junta. "The Directorio," emphasized Zoila Mullet, "wanted to maintain its independence." [22]

Most prominent, perhaps, of these anti-Machado groups was the ABC, a clandestine organization composed of intellectuals, students, and the middle sectors of society. Led by several intellectuals who were Harvard graduates, the ABC undermined Machado's position through sabotage and terroristic actions, and in December, 1932, published a manifesto in Havana criticizing the underlying structure of Cuban society and outlining a detailed program of economic and political reforms.[23]

A group of Directorio leaders maintained close contact with the ABC. Older ABC leaders often used the courageous youngsters to perform terroristic acts, supplying them with needed weapons and money. "Several bomb explosions and the assault on the army depot in Santiago de Cuba," claimed Directorio leader Eduardo Chibás, "were actions that although carried out by the students, were credited to the ABC, thus enhancing the organization's prestige." [24] The two groups severed their relations, just prior to Machado's downfall, when the ABC supported United States Envoy Benjamin Sumner Welles' mediation efforts while the Directorio opposed them.

Late in 1932 the ABC drew up a two-phase plan to eliminate Machado. Students were to play only a minor role in the plan. The first phase consisted in assassinating a prominent government official, and the second in blowing up the Havana cemetery during the official's funeral, thus killing all top government leaders, including Machado. The first part of the plan was completed on September 28, 1932, when ABC members fired on and killed Senate President Clemente Vázquez Bello near Havana's Country Club suburb. The second part, however, failed when the government ordered Vázquez Bello's funeral to take place in Santa Clara, his hometown in Las Villas Province, and a gardener working at the cemetery discovered the buried explosives.[25]

Vázquez Bello's assassination cost Machado's opposition dearly. Police raided secret meeting places, arresting students and ABC leaders, whom they tortured and killed under the *ley de fuga.** Those students and oppositionist leaders not captured or driven into exile lived in a continuous state of terror. They were persecuted and, in many instances, finally hunted down in their various hiding places and assassinated by Machado's porra.[26]

This was the existing condition in the island when the United States, attempting to find a peaceful solution to Cuba's political situation, sent its Special Envoy Benjamin Sumner Welles to act as mediator between government and opposition.[27] The mediation was supported by most political factions and leaders, with the exception of the Conservative followers of former President Menocal and the Directorio. Menocal declared that the mediation had led to the dissolution of the Revolutionary Junta functioning in New York, thus destroying the unity of the anti-Machado opposition. "It is impossible for the Machado government," he asserted, "to give life to a succeeding government without branding it with its own vices."[28]

The Directorio also opposed the mediation. Claiming that the student movement was directed not only toward Machado's overthrow but also "toward promoting a thorough cleansing of the system," the Directorio denounced the mediation as "tacitly implying an intervention by the coercive powers of the American government." [29] Cuba's distinguished writer and his-

---

* This was not a law, but rather the name applied to Machado's police method of killing prisoners while "trying to escape."

torian, Juan J. Remos, explained to the author that the students opposed any compromise with Machado and declared that they would reject any solution resulting from United States mediation.[30]

The struggle to overthrow Machado had acquired new dimensions with United States involvement. The leaders of the generation of 1930 saw themselves as representatives of the national will and heirs to Martí's legacy whose mission was to carry on the revolution that the United States had frustrated in 1898. Opposing American supervision of Cuban affairs and the humiliating Platt Amendment, they found inspiration and guidance in Martí's teachings. Martí's vision for a just society in a politically and economically independent nation became their creed.

The members of the generation of 1930 were generally very young. Most of the student leaders were in their early twenties. A majority came from middle-class backgrounds. Some, like Eduardo Chibás, however, were from wealthy families, while others, like Sánchez Arango, came from poorer homes. Several were descendants of veterans of the wars of independence. Their ancestors' participation in public affairs seemed to have been an inspiration for their own active political roles. Many came from areas outside of the capital city. Living apart from families and parental discipline and exposed to the loneliness of a new environment, these students gravitated toward the campus and were perhaps more prone to political involvement than the average city student. Coming from the countryside where social and economic stratification was accentuated, they contrasted life in the provinces and the capital. While some soon forgot their background and became "assimilated," others found the contrast shocking and attempted to bridge the gap between the two areas.

Originally the Directorio leaders had no program beyond eliminating Machado. Machado's removal was considered the panacea that would cure all of Cuba's ills. As time went on, however, several factors heightened both their convictions and political sophistication. Some students who spent their exile in the United States returned to Cuba with ideas suggested by Franklin Delano Roosevelt's New Deal. The American evolutionary experiment in social justice with freedom exerted strong influence. Others who lived in Europe came in contact with Communist or Fascist ideology, or with the social and economic ideas of the Spanish Republic. Still others became impregnated with the ABC ideology. Students told a United States correspondent visiting Havana in September, 1933, that their movement "compared most closely with the new revolutionary Spanish Republic." [31] The students read a variety of authors, including Argentina's José Ingenieros, Uruguay's José E. Rodó, Mexico's José Vasconcelos, Cuba's José Martí and Enrique José Varona, and Spain's Francisco Giner de los Ríos, Miguel de Unamuno, and José Ortega y Gasset.[32] The Spanish generation of 1898, with its humane, spiritual, and tolerant ideas, strongly influenced the Cuban generation of 1930. [33]

The Directorio leaders advocated several reforms. They wanted not only to overthrow Machado but also to wipe out all vestiges of his regime, including corrupt pro-Machado army officers, politicians, office holders, and university professors. They called for a complete reorganization of Cuba's economic structure, including revision of the foreign debt, tax reforms, and a national banking and currency system removing Cuba from monetary and financial dependence upon the United States. Aware that the Platt Amendment would only allow for continuous United States interference, they wanted its removal. The students also demanded agrarian reform and eventual nationalization of the sugar and mining industries. Finally, they wanted an autonomous university, sheltered from political interference.[34]

Sumner Welles' mediation efforts culminated in a general strike and an army revolt, which forced Machado to leave the country on August 12, 1933. [35] It is interesting to note that this general strike deepened the schism between the Cuban Communist Party and the anti-Machado groups. Although the party played an important role in promoting the general strike, it backed down just prior to Machado's fall and issued a back-to-work order. Afraid that the general strike might provoke United States intervention or the establishment of a pro-United States government, the Communists changed tactics at the last minute. Communist Party leader César Vilar visited Machado and reached an agreement with the dictator, obtaining concessions for the party in return for calling off the strike.[36]

The Communists' back-to-work order was obeyed by few workers. The party's lack of organization prevented the order from filtering down to the lower ranks, and the increasing excitement precluded the following of such a radical turn. The pact with Machado discredited the Communists, especially among the students who found it hard to condone their shifting tactics. From that time on, the party, alienated from progressive and revolutionary forces within the country, found it easier to reach agreements and work with traditional conservative political parties and governments, even with military presidents.[37]

THE CÉSPEDES INTERREGNUM

Machado was succeeded by Carlos Manuel de Céspedes, son of Cuba's first president during the rebellion against Spain in the 1860's. A prestigious although uninspiring figure, Céspedes soon received United States support and the backing of most anti-Machado groups.[38] He annulled Machado's constitutional amendments of 1928, restored the 1901 Constitution, and prepared to bring the country back to normalcy.

Returning Cuba to normalcy seemed an almost impossible task at the time. The deepening economic depression had worsened the people's misery, and Machado's overthrow had released a wave of uncontrolled anger and anxiety. Looting and disorder were widespread in Havana, where armed bands sought out and executed Machado's henchmen.[39] In rural areas, discontented peasants took over sugar mills and threatened wealthy landowners. The worldwide chaos of the early 1930's seemed to have spread to Cuba.

Machado's overthrow, furthermore, marked the beginning of an era of reform. The revolutionary wave that swept away the dictatorship had acquired the characteristics of a major revolution. Although lacking a defined ideology, this revolution was clearly aimed at transforming all phases of national life. The leaders of the generation of 1930 were the best exponents of this reformist zeal. By espousing usual Communist propaganda issues, such as anti-Americanism and nonintervention, and by advocating measures of social and economic significance for the less privileged sectors of society, the students monopolized the rhetoric of revolution.[40]

To them the Céspedes regime represented an attempt to slow down the reformist process that had been gaining momentum since the 1920's. Considering the regime a product of the mediation and a tool of the United States, the Directorio soon manifested its relentless opposition to Céspedes' rule. Céspedes' refusal to abrogate the 1901 Constitution, which the students regarded as too closely modeled after the United States Constitution and ill-adapted to Cuba's cultural milieu, created a crisis. The Directorio demanded a constitutional convention. In their desire for a new constitution, the students evidenced the same faith as earlier Latin American leaders in constitutions as the panaceas that could solve their countries' difficulties. The Directorio, furthermore, linked Céspedes to the deposed dictator, blaming him for serving in Machado's first Cabinet and for living abroad as a diplomat. Finally, the students accused the regime of "softness with porristas" and of failing to confiscate the huge fortunes of the dictator's followers.[41]

THE STUDENTS AND BATISTA

By September, 1933, a new source of unrest entered Cuba's political picture. Unhappy with both a proposed reduction in

pay and an order restricting their promotions, the lower eche-
lons of the army, led by sergeant-stenographer Fulgencio Batista, met at Camp Columbia in Havana on September 4 and
invited the Directorio to this meeting. Batista's contact with
Directorio leaders dated back to the anti-Machado struggle
when he had served as stenographer during some of the student's trials.

By the time the students arrived at Camp Columbia, army
discipline had collapsed. Sergeants were in command and had
arrested numerous army officers. Carlos Prío Socarrás, one of
the first students to arrive at Camp Columbia on the eve of
September 4, reported that the sergeants were still undecided
whether or not to overthrow the civilian government.[42] After
consulting with Batista and the army, the Directorio agreed to
Céspedes' overthrow and named five men to form a pentarchy
(a five-member executive commission) to head a provisional
government.[43] Two university professors, Dr. Grau San Martín and Dr. Guillermo Portela, journalist Sergio Carbó, and
a lawyer and intellectual, José M. Irisarri, were immediately
appointed. Directorio leader Prío Socarrás suggested Batista
for the fifth member, but Batista declined and the choice finally
fell on Profirio Franca, a prestigious banker and financier.[44]

September 4, 1933, was a turning point in Cuba's history.
That date marked the army's entrance as an organized force
into politics and Batista's emergence as the arbiter of Cuba's
destiny for years to come. On that date the students and the
military, two armed groups accustomed to violence, united to
rule Cuba. "September 4," wrote one of the members of the
Pentarchy, "is the legitimate child of September 30 [the date
when the Directorio was founded] . . . the most sincere homage
of the military barracks to the University." [45] That homage,
however, was short-lived. A contest soon began between students and military for supremacy. There were very few who
expected the students to win.

The Pentarchy's inability to rule the country became evident
at once. The group lacked not only the support of the various
political parties and groups, but also of the United States. The

Roosevelt administration, surprised and confused by events in the island, rushed naval vessels to Cuban waters and refused to recognize the five-man government. When one member of the Pentarchy promoted sergeant Batista to the rank of colonel without the required approval of the other four, another member resigned and the regime collapsed. In a meeting with Batista and the army on September 10, 1933, the Directorio appointed Dr. Ramón Grau San Martín as Provisional President.[46]

The new president had no political experience to qualify him for the job at such a crucial time. He had won the admiration of the students when in 1928 he allowed the expelled Directorio leaders to read their manifesto to his class. At a time when other professors refused the students' request, Grau's gesture gained for him a following at the University. While in jail in 1931, students and Grau met again and cemented their relationship. When the Pentarchy collapsed, their old professor was the students' first choice.

STUDENTS IN POWER:
A FRUSTRATED REVOLUTION

With Grau, the generation of 1930 was catapulted into power. The students held Cuba's destiny in their hands. It was a unique spectacle indeed. Amidst thunder from the left and the right, and opposition from most political parties and personalities, the Directorio held daily meetings to shape governmental policy. An American newspaperman attending one of these meetings reported that the students regarded their government "as a non-Communist leftist dictatorship." [47]

Grau's regime was the high-water mark of the revolutionary process and of the radical nationalism of the generation of 1930. Nationalist sentiment rather than radical doctrines dominated the regime's consideration of economic questions. The government was pro-labor, opposing the predominance of foreign capital. Soon after coming to power, Grau abrogated the 1901 Constitution, promulgated provisional statutes to govern Cuba, and called for a constitutional convention with elections subsequently set for April 1, 1934. [48] He also began negotiations for the abrogation of the Platt Amendment.[49] Grau took immediate action to eliminate Machado's followers from government positions and appointed commissioners to "purge" government offices. Since the dictatorship had captured the machinery of the old political parties, Grau issued a decree dissolving them. On October 6 the government complied with one of the oldest demands of the university reform movement by granting the University of Havana its autonomy from government control.[50]

Faced with a mounting wave of strikes and social unrest, Grau implemented a popular and reformist program. On September 20 he issued a decree establishing a maximum working day of eight hours.[51] On November 7 the government issued a decree on labor organization which sought to "Cubanize" the labor movement and restrict Communist influences by limiting the role of foreign leaders. It required Cuban citizenship of all union officials, and all labor organizations were ordered to register with the Labor Department. On the following day Grau signed the Nationalization of Labor decree, popularly known as the "50 Percent Law." This law required all industrial, commercial, and agricultural enterprises to employ native Cubans for at least half of their total working force (excepting only managers and technicians who could not be supplanted by natives), and to pay half of the total payroll to Cubans. While these two laws gained much labor support for the government and diminished Communist influence in the unions, they also alienated the many Spaniards and other foreign minority groups living in Cuba.

Grau's measures[52] also aroused American hostility. The United States viewed the unrest in Cuba and Grau's failure to win support from the various political factions with much concern. The overthrow of the United States-backed Céspedes regime was undoubtedly a defeat for Roosevelt's policy toward Cuba in general and for Ambassador Sumner Welles' mediation efforts in particular. Relations were strained by the Directorio's charge that the American Ambassador had gathered at the National Hotel 300 ex-officers to plan governmental subversion and subsequent intervention by United States marines. A temporary improvement occurred when Sumner Welles held a meeting with the students and assured them that the Cuban government would not be barred from recognition either because of its revolutionary origin or its radical program. Sumner Welles denied, furthermore, any hostile bias toward the Grau regime.[53] But Grau's seizure of two American-owned sugar mills, which had been closed down because of labor troubles, and his temporary take over of the Cuban Electric Company because of rate disputes and additional labor problems, increased Washington's apprehension.

Lack of recognition by the United States complicated the many problems facing Grau. Since recognition was considered by Cuban political leaders as a key factor for the existence of any Cuban government, United States policy condemned the Grau regime and encouraged opposition groups and rebellious army officers. Opposition was strongest from the Communists, the displaced army officers, and the ABC. Student leader Eddy Chibás bitterly complained that while the Directorio never used terrorism against the ABC-backed Céspedes regime, the ABC used it to combat Grau's government.[54] A Communist-supported demonstration honoring Mella on September 29 led to a clash with the army in which six persons were killed and many others wounded. The army retaliated by raiding the headquarters of the National Confederation of Labor and the Anti-Imperialist League, burning furniture and Communist literature.[55]

This government attack on the Communists was followed by a confrontation with the army officers and the ABC. Former army officers had taken refuge in the National Hotel—where Ambassador Sumner Welles resided—and prepared to fight against the regime. On October 2 the army began a bombardment of the hotel. By that time Sumner Welles had moved out. The battle of the National Hotel lasted several hours, until finally the officers surrendered. As the officers were being removed from the hotel, an unexpected shot precipitated panic among the soldiers and several officers were slaughtered. On November 8, rebel forces backed by the ABC and recruited from the army, police, and civilians seized Atarés Fortress and various other strongholds in Havana. This revolt was also crushed, but only after a two-day battle.[56] Although these victories consolidated the government, they also strengthened Batista and the army's influence. Sánchez Arango told the author that Batista's power had grown so much that as early as November, 1933, he began conspiring to overthrow Grau's regime.[57]

The government's inner conflict contributed to its instability. A faction led by student leader and Interior Minister Antonio Guiteras advocated a continuation of the program of social reform. Strongly nationalistic and sincerely motivated, Guiteras initiated much of the regime's legislation, and many considered him the real brains behind Grau.[58] Another faction controlled by Batista and the army wanted a conservative program that would bring about United States recognition. Grau seemed to have been caught in the middle of these conflicting forces. On November 6, the Directorio, feeling that its mandate had expired, declared itself dissolved, announcing, however, that its members would continue to support President Grau.[59] On January 6 an assembly of university students opposing the ascending military role within the government, and angered over the killing of a student, withdrew their support from the Grau administration.[60]

By January it became evident that the regime would soon collapse. Student support was rapidly waning. The military conspired to take power. Washington refused to recognize a regime that threatened its vested interests in the island. Industrial and commercial leaders opposed Grau's legislation. Fearing that the government's program would attract labor support, the Communists violently attacked Grau. A national teachers' strike for better wages also aggravated an already unstable situation. On January 14, 1934, Army Chief Fulgencio Batista forced President Grau to resign. After a two-day rule by engineer Carlos Hevia, Batista appointed Carlos Mendieta as Cuba's Provisional President. Within five days after Mendieta's accession to power, the United States recognized Cuba's new government. "Batista's acceptance of Hevia," wrote Rubén de León, "was not sincere since he had already agreed with Caffrey [United States Ambassador Jefferson Caffrey, who succeeded Sumner Welles] to appoint Mendieta . . . Batista betrayed not only the revolution but the revolutionaries whom he had promised he would support Hevia." [61] From exile Grau bitterly criticized Batista and the United States. "The deciding factor which led to my final resignation," he wrote, "aside from the perturbing influence of illegitimate interests and the handiwork of Mr. Caffrey, was my refusal to grant an extension of military jurisdiction repeatedly requested by the head of the army [Batista], which would have prevented ordinary courts of justice from judging common crimes committed by members of the armed forces." [62]

3
Politization of
the Student Movement

In the years following Grau's overthrow, the generation of
1930 experienced the harsh facts of Cuba's power politics.
The students thought that Machado's overthrow would signal
the beginning of a new era of morality and change. They
learned better. Dominated by the army, Cuba's political life
returned to its traditional course. To govern Cuba, Batista
chose as allies the old generation of politicians expelled from
power with Machado. Opportunistic and unscrupulous individuals assumed important government positions, corruption
continued, repression and terrorism flourished. The years of
struggling and suffering seemed in vain.

Students felt disillusioned and frustrated. Some abandoned
their earlier idealism to find comfort in professional and business ventures. Others departed for foreign lands, never to return to their tragic island. Still others accepted radical ideologies such as communism or fascism. Several, however, broke
with their past and shared in the spoils of office. Desiring to
continue fighting for their frustrated revolution, many organized or joined the Partido Revolucionario Cubano (Auténtico) in February of 1934. [1]

Taking their name from Martí's Partido Revolucionario Cubano of 1892, this group became the repository of revolu-

tionary virtue. Directorio leaders joined the new party and appointed as its president Grau San Martín, then living in Mexican exile. The party's program called for economic and political nationalism, social justice, and civil liberties, and emphasized the right of Cubans to share more fully in the country's economic resources. Although the party's program was silent on the question of peaceful or forceful methods of achieving power, Grau seemed at first to favor peaceful opposition to Mendieta and Batista.

STUDENTS AGAINST BATISTA: THE OPPOSITION FAILS

The opposition of some to the use of violence split the generation of 1930. Believing that the best strategy to fight Batista was the use of violence, Grau's former Interior Minister, Antonio Guiteras, founded the Joven Cuba, a clandestine revolutionary organization. Batista's most militant opponents joined the organization. Joven Cuba continued those tactics of urban violence employed so successfully against Machado. Terrorism flared; bombs exploded daily, sabotage crippled electric power. The violence of the Machado days reappeared with unabated strength.

Students were particularly active against the Mendieta government. Early in 1934 the University of Havana was reopened after three years of suspended classes. Demonstrations soon followed. In April, a policeman and a student were wounded during a protest over the arrest of several fellow students.[2] In May, the death of a University of Havana student produced a short-lived though widespread student strike.[3] Mendieta's failure to guarantee the University's autonomy increased student opposition, leading to another strike. The government finally yielded to student pressure, issuing a decree restoring university autonomy and the funds from the national revenue originally provided for by Grau.[4] By midyear, however, the University was in turmoil again as students considered charges against forty-five professors accused of taking part in the disciplinary councils of 1927 and 1928. Allegedly, these same professors had collected salaries from the Machado government during the years the University had been closed. Following turbulent days, the whole University faculty resigned on June 29. But the University Council, the highest administrative body of the University, composed of members elected by each of the three faculties, refused to accept the resignation of those professors who were in agreement with the students.[5] This refusal preserved a skeleton faculty allowing for a rapid reorganization.[6]

With autonomy as a sheltering device and with almost total control of university affairs, student hostility toward Mendieta and Batista increased. On September 19, the students announced their determination to combat the regime with every means at their disposal. The students demanded repeal of the Public Order Law and full reestablishment of all constitutional guarantees; subjection of the military to civil authority; immediate punishment of soldiers accused of having killed a university student; repeal of the constitutional provision prohibiting the confiscation of property from Machado's followers; and, finally, withdrawal of all troops from educational institutions.[7] On the thirtieth of that same month more than thirty bombs exploded in Havana alone. Several students were also wounded when police dispersed gatherings commemorating Trejo's death.[8] In another demonstration in Havana, a student leader was seriously wounded.[9]

Labor unrest and Auténtico opposition added a grim note to an already unstable situation. Throughout 1934 and early 1935, approximately 100 strikes occurred throughout the island. Discontent in the sugar mills was widespread. The Auténticos repeatedly condemned the regime. In a September 11, 1934, public manifesto they requested elections, pointing out that the most important development of the year had been "the tremendous growth in military influence." They demanded a return to civilian-constitutional government and the trial of the military guard under whose escort two students were slain. The appeal also called on professional men, students, and workers who opposed army control "to align themselves with the party." [10]

Opposition to the government culminated in a general strike in March, 1935. Although it began when elementary school teachers protested the government's neglect of education, it soon spread to other sectors of society throughout the country, acquiring a political character. University of Havana students organized a strike committee, appealing to the people to join the movement.[11] Criticizing the government's inability to restore social and political peace, the University Council soon voted to support the students.[12] Labor followed suit and joined the strikers. One factor precipitating the strike was the breakup of the coalition supporting Mendieta. First the Menocalistas left the government. Next was the ABC, which complained it had not received its promised share of authority. Then prominent Cabinet members resigned, weakening the people's confidence in the regime. This confidence reached a low ebb when the government's Finance Minister was accused of embezzling public funds.

Mendieta bitterly criticized the strike, claiming that it was directed against wealth and property, peace and order, and even the Cuban family.[13] Fearing that the movement might topple the regime, Batista threw the army's full weight against the strikers. Students and labor leaders were persecuted, imprisoned, or assassinated. Unions were dissolved. The University of Havana was closed and occupied by the military.[14] After several days of struggle, the backbone of the movement was broken.

Repression, however, continued. On May 8, Batista eliminated his most bitter opponent, Antonio Guiteras. While waiting in Matanzas Province for a boat to escape to the United States, Guiteras was betrayed by one of his associates and killed in an encounter with government forces.[15] During previous months, military firing squads, for the first time in the

history of the Cuban Republic, had executed two civilians—
Jaime Greinstein and José Castiello. Although they were accused by the government of terrorism, their only crime had
been to oppose Batista.

The failure of the strike consolidated the regime. In the
years that followed, Cuba's political life was all but dominated
by Batista and the army. Until 1940 Batista ruled through
puppet presidents, among whom the chief incumbents were
Mendieta (1934–1935), José A. Barnet (1935–1936), Miguel Mariano Gómez (1936), and Federico Laredo Brú
(1936–1940). Desiring to win popular support and to rival
the Auténticos, Batista imitated his Mexican counterpart,
General Lázaro Cárdenas, by sponsoring an impressive body
of welfare legislation. Public administration, health, sanita-
tion, education, and public works improved. Workers were
allowed to unionize and organize the Confederation of Cuban
Workers. Legislation to provide pensions, insurance, limited
working hours, and minimum wages largely satisfied the workers' demands. Batista maintained tight political control until
1940, when he officially assumed the chief executive office,
securing his election through a coalition of political parties
that included the Communists.

The collapse of the strike, the closing of the University of
Havana, and the ruthless repression that followed almost completely ended student political involvement. Even after the
University reopened in 1937, there was little student activism.
With most of the leaders of the generation of 1930 in exile and
therefore unable to provide needed leadership, and with the
regime clamping down on opposition, students followed a less
militant path. Batista's and the army's method of dosing rebellious students with castor oil also seemed to dampen student ardor.

Other factors were also important in containing student
activism in the late 1930's. The disillusionment that followed
the "frustrated revolution" promoted among the students a
more cynical attitude toward politics. The early idealism of the
generation of 1930 was less evident now among new student

leaders. Then, the more conciliatory policy followed by President-elect Gómez and by his Vice-President and successor, Laredo Brú, generated a cordial climate. Laredo Brú allowed for the return of political exiles, avoided repressive measures against the students, guaranteed the University's autonomy, and called for the drafting of a new constitution. With elections for a constitutional convention and for a new president in sight, politics took a more normal course, and students now felt that the need for violence had diminished. Aware that violence would not bring him to power, Grau himself returned from exile and engaged in electoral practices, thus legitimatizing the Batista supported regimes.

The constitutional convention convened in Havana in early 1940. With only fifty-seven percent of the eligible voters participating, government parties won 558,000 votes, but only thirty-five delegates; the opposition parties won 551,000 votes and placed forty-one delegates.[16] Several leaders of the generation of 1930, such as Eduardo Chibás, Carlos Prío Socarrás, and others, were elected as delegates. Grau San Martín was chosen president of the assembly. Despite pressure from both right and left, work went smoothly, with Batista and Grau competing for popular support. But when Batista and former President Menocal signed a political pact that left oppositionist groups in a minority position in the assembly, Grau resigned.[17] The Constitution, however, was soon completed and proclaimed that same year.

The Constitution was in many respects the embodiment of the aspirations of the generation of 1930. The president was to serve only one term, though he might be reelected after eight years. Many civil liberties and social welfare provisions were defined at great length. Workers were guaranteed paid vacations, minimum wages, and job tenure. Cuban nationals were to be favored over foreigners in the establishment of new industries. The University of Havana's autonomy received constitutional sanction in Article 53. The convention thus fulfilled one of the oldest demands of the students.[18]

Batista was the first president elected under the new Constitution. Supported by a coalition of political parties, and by the Communists, he defeated his old rival Grau San Martín. Batista's administration coincided with World War II, and Cuba collaborated closely with the United States, declaring war on the Axis powers in 1941.

Throughout the war years, the students supported the Allied war effort and avoided demonstrating against the pro-United States Batista government. In July, 1942, the Federation of University Students (FEU), organized after the University reopened back in 1937, demanded that Batista form an honest, efficient, war cabinet prior to registration for obligatory military service. Declaring that students originally proposed this service and reiterating their support of the Allies, FEU spokesmen requested competent army officers, creation of military schools, and obligatory military service without exclusions or privileges.[19]

In a meeting held at the University of Havana that same month and attended by several thousand students and by Grau, student leaders criticized the Communists' anti-war posture and their tactical shift after Russia joined the Allies. FEU President Octavio Hernández said that "while the Federation called for national mobilization and military service, the Communists were claiming that Cubans repudiated the war and that it was an imperialist war." [20] Students also attacked the government. Explaining that they wanted a new era of morality and decency, FEU speakers criticized the corruption and disorganization of the Batista administration.[21]

STUDENT ACTIVISM AND
URBAN VIOLENCE

By this time signs of a social phenomenon appeared that later permeated Cuban politics and especially student politics. Whereas prior to Machado's rule uprisings in the countryside and guerrilla fighting had been common, during the anti-Machado insurrection urban terrorism and violence had been successfully employed. This pattern of violence evident then at the national level reappeared now at the local level, mainly in urban areas. This time groups employing violence organized not only to mobilize political power and influence governmental policies, but also for other purposes. These ranged considerably, from punishing Machado's supporters who had escaped "revolutionary justice" to obtaining government privileges and subsidies, influencing the appointment of personnel, and securing university degrees with little or no study. Rivalries among gangs led to frequent street fighting and vendettas.

Batista's tight political control and the events of World War II prevented the growth of these groups. Some incidents of violence, however, occurred in the late 1930's and early 1940's. The most notorious, perhaps, were two unsuccessful assassination attempts, one on the life of Chibás in November, 1939, and another on Orestes Ferrara, in March, 1943. Ferrara was an old Machado supporter and had been elected to the 1940 constitutional convention.[22]

With the end of World War II and the coming to power of Grau and the Auténticos in 1944, organized use of violence took on an unprecedented dimension. The relative calm of the war years suddenly ended, giving way to a violent and materialistic era. Urban violence, a legacy of the early 1930's, reappeared now with tragic proportions. Although part of the generation that emerged out of World War II retained a redemptionist fanaticism and a desire to fulfill the aspirations of "the frustrated revolution," a still larger part evidenced an insatiable appetite for power and wealth, and a determination to obtain both regardless of obstacles. Violence-prone refugees of the Spanish Civil War also extended their activism and rivalries to Cuba. An explanation often given for the rise of these violent gangs during this period is the fact that they opposed Communist domination in labor unions and in the University of Havana. While their anti-Communist character seems undeniable, an explanation of this phenomenon in terms of anti-Communism alone seems borne out of present-day thinking, rather than out of the reality of Cuba's politics in the 1930's and 1940's.

Elected to the presidency in 1944, Grau followed a conciliatory policy toward these groups and permitted their proliferation, in many instances placing their leaders on government payrolls. There were various reasons for Grau's acquiescence. First, several of the gang leaders had participated in the anti-Machado struggle and had maintained close contact with the Auténticos. Grau was unwilling now to face his old friends, the "boys," as he used to call them. Then, unable to count on the support of the Batista-oriented military, Grau's appointees organized private armies to protect their areas of graft and privilege. These armies, furthermore, helped to implement Auténtico decrees and to expel the Communists from control in the labor unions. Finally, fearing the power of these gangs and their trouble-making capabilities if employed against the government, Grau allowed them almost complete freedom of action. Aureliano Sánchez Arango explained that "José M. Alemán, Grau's Minister of Education, placed these *pistoleros* [gangsters] on the payroll of [his] Ministry, allocating $80,-000 for their maintenance." [23] When in September, 1946, a militant gang assassinated the son of another minister, an outraged Grau complained that he had done everything possible for a tolerant government. "In the Ministry of Education," he added cynically, "there is a payroll devoted especially to support these gangsters. But I cannot permit one of my collaborators to be attacked in this manner." [24]

This situation continued under the presidency of Grau's protégé, Carlos Prío Socarrás. Elected in 1948, the former Directorio leader also avoided confronting his old friends and continued his predecessor's mild policies. With the appointment of Sánchez Arango as Minister of Education, however, the end of the pistoleros seemed to have arrived. Sánchez Arango eliminated them from the payroll and "cleaned up" his ministry. "But my efforts," claims Sánchez Arango, "were not successful, for Prío soon placed the gangsters on the payroll of the Ministry of Finance." [25]

The three most prominent groups operating in Cuba were the ARG (Acción Revolucionaria Guiteras), the MSR (Movimiento Socialista Revolucionario), and the UIR (Unión Insurreccional Revolucionaria). Some members of these organizations belonged to the generation of 1930, and several had participated in the Spanish Civil War or World War II. ARG activists were originally linked to the Grau revolutionary government of 1933 and to Guiteras' Joven Cuba. One of the MSR leaders, Rolando Masferrer, fought on the Communist side during the Spanish Civil War. After returning to Cuba, he broke with the Communists, was elected to Congress on the Liberal Party ticket, and helped organize the MSR. "Masferrer," claims L. Ricardo Alonso, "was a known gangster and a dreaded figure." [26] The UIR leader, Emilio Tró, fought with United States forces in the Pacific and after he returned to Cuba, Grau appointed him Director of the National Police Academy. This job put him in a position of strength and provided the necessary protection for his activities. Not only Tró, but also other leaders of action groups, such as Mario Salabarría, head of the rival MSR, were appointed to important posts within the police department. In a 1947 interview, Tró claimed that his group's objective was the punishment of Machado and Batista henchmen. Calling for honesty, real social justice for peasants and workers, and a socialized economy, Tró pointed out that his organization was against both Batista and the Communists.[27]

These pistoleros found sanctuary and allies at the University of Havana. The University's autonomy, which prohibited police from entering the campus, afforded a safe emplacement for their activities. Although most of them were nonstudents some student leaders joined the gangs. Others acted on their own, using their influence and toughness in student politics. Still others sold their services to the highest bidder. The prestige associated with being a student leader was used by unscrupulous individuals to further their political aspirations and obtain government positions for friends and relatives. The presidency of the FEU degenerated into a stepping-stone for political prominence. Within the University a position of leadership allowed such a student to pass courses with little or no studying. Faculty and administrators fell prey to this elite of campus politicians, professional students, and gangsters. The memory of Ramiro Valdés Daussá, the Directorio leader and professor assassinated for attempting to curb gangsterism at the University, was still fresh in the minds of many. Respect and order reached a low ebb. An interesting example of university life was afforded by the president of the Student Association of the School of Agronomical Engineering. This student moved his wife and children to a University cottage at the school's botanical gardens, brought to the campus a cow and several goats, and lived in full comfort.[28] The University itself was penetrated by graft and corruption. Cuba's distinguished writer and historian, Juan J. Remos, blames Grau for corrupting youth with political bribing.[29]

The organized use of force became one of the main characteristics of student politics. Rivalries between the UIR and MSR were particularly strong. In February, 1948, former FEU President and MSR leader Manolo Castro was assassinated in Havana. His death led to the assassination of two students, supposedly for having participated in the shooting of a University policeman friend of the murdered FEU leader.[30] Early in 1949, a faculty session of the School of Social Sciences was interrupted by a fusillade of shots. In April, FEU Vice-President Justo Fuentes was shot and killed in Havana.[31] Violating the University's autonomy, police penetrated into the campus in September, confiscated a large cache of arms that included machine guns and thousands of bullets, and arrested several students.[32] On September 20, Gustavo Mejías, president of the student association of the School of Sciences and an opponent of the *bonches* (as the student armed bands were called), was shot to death at the University's swimming club.[33] The widespread activities of the bonches led the Cuban daily *El Mundo* to declare editorially:

> ... violence holds sway at the University. Professors and students are nothing but the evident prisoners of a few groups of desperadoes who impose their will

and pass their examinations at pistol point. The University Council itself has declared its inability to repress these gangs for lack of coercive powers.[34]

FIDEL CASTRO:
THE UNIVERSITY STUDENT

It was in this environment that Fidel Castro and other leaders received their first schooling in politics. While studying law at the University of Havana in the late 1940's, Fidel participated in the activities of student gangs and associated closely with UIR leaders.[35] Although police files implicated him in the murder of rival student leader Manolo Castro in 1948 and in other violent actions, nothing was proved. Fidel soon acquired a reputation for personal ambition, forcefulness, and fine oratory. Yet, he never became a prominent student leader. On several occasions he was defeated in student elections or prevented from winning by the nature of student politics. Perhaps his unhappy experiences at the University created in him the dislike for elections he evidenced after coming to power.

In 1947 Fidel enrolled in an abortive expedition against Dominican Republic Dictator Rafael Leónidas Trujillo. The expeditionary force was allegedly financed by the Grau government and supported by the FEU. Manolo Castro, Rolando Masferrer, and other MSR members were deeply involved. A Dominican general, backed by exile Dominican leader Juan Bosch, commanded the forces. Training was held at Cayo Confites in eastern Cuba. Desiring to participate in the venture, Fidel contacted FEU President Enrique Ovares. In a training camp where his political rivals were in charge, Fidel feared for his life and wanted Ovares to negotiate a truce with the MSR leaders. Fidel was allowed to join, but soon the Cuban government, pressured by several Latin American nations and the United States, called off the expedition. While the expeditionaries were being taken back to Nuevitas Bay in a

Cuban navy frigate, Fidel jumped overboard and swam ashore. "Castro," says Ovares, "was afraid that Masferrer would try to kill him now that the truce was over. His action, furthermore, made for good publicity." [36]

One of the most controversial episodes of Fidel Castro's student life was his participation in the "Bogotazo"—the Bogotá riots following the assassination of Liberal Party leader Jorge Eliecer Gaitán in April, 1948. Following a schism within the International Union of Students (UIE), the FEU began organizing a Latin American Union of Students. The new movement was financed by Juan D. Perón. The Argentinian dictator favored the establishment of an anti-colonialist—anti-imperialist Latin American Student Union under his control. Opposing the Ninth Inter-American Conference scheduled to meet in Bogotá, Perón suggested that the FEU have a preliminary meeting of Latin American students in Bogotá to coincide with the conference. [37] Not only Perón, but also the Communists were bent on disrupting the Inter-American Conference.

FEU president Enrique Ovares, Fidel Castro, Rafael del Pino, and Alfredo Guevara represented the Cuban students. [38] Ovares explained to the author that Fidel had to leave Cuba earlier, for the MSR had accused him of being involved in Manolo Castro's assassination. After traveling to Venezuela, Fidel met his colleagues in Bogotá. Ovares recalls that Fidel, claiming that it would be good for his political future, asked to preside over the student meeting. But despite Castro's pleadings, Ovares insisted on presiding himself. The two students attempted to visit Gaitán and to ask him to deliver the closing speech at their meeting. [39]

Gaitán, however, did not live to deliver the speech. Shortly before his meeting with the Cuban students, he was assassinated. His death unleashed a wave of anger against the Conservative regime of President Mariano Ospina Pérez. Riots and chaos followed. Fidel was caught up in the violence that rocked Colombian society. Picking up a rifle from a police station, he joined the mobs and roamed through the streets distributing anti-United States propaganda and inciting the populace to revolt. Ovares is still puzzled by Castro's conduct. "When I found him several hours later carrying the rifle," says Ovares, "I asked him what he was doing. Fidel only responded that it was his duty." [40] For some, Castro's actions evidenced his link with international communism, while for others it was just a coincidence. Ovares emphatically denies that Fidel was a Communist agent. "It was," he claims, "a hysteric, ambitious, and uncontrollable Fidel who acted in those events." [41] Pursued by the Colombian government for their participation in the riots, the students sought asylum in the Cuban Embassy and were later flown back to Havana.

Student politics was only a microcosm of Cuba's political life. An entire system of nepotism, favoritism, and gangsterism predominated. Despite numerous accomplishments, the Auténticos failed to provide the country with an honest government or to diversify Cuba's one-crop economy.[42] The reformist zeal evident during Grau's first administration had diminished considerably in the intervening decade. Grau himself seemed softened after years of exile and frustration. He faced, furthermore, determined opposition in Congress and from conservative elements that had joined the party. Not only Grau, but many of the old student leaders of the generation of 1930 shared in the spoils of office. When confronted with the reality of Cuban politics, their early idealism and reformism gave way to materialism and opportunism.

For many, the Auténticos had failed to fulfill the aspirations of the anti-Machado revolution, especially in the area of administrative honesty.[43] Perhaps the Cubans expected too much too soon. The rapid reforms implemented during Grau's first admininstration were still remembered and the people expected their continuation.

Grau's failure to bring honesty and order to Cuba's public life, and the presidential aspirations of Auténtico Congressman Eduardo Chibás, produced a rift in the party. Chibás and other Auténtico leaders formed the Partido del Pueblo Cubano (Ortodoxo) in 1947. Led by Chibás, a former student leader of the generation of 1930, this party became the repository of the ideals of the "frustrated revolution" and the refuge of a new generation, determined to transform those ideals into reality. Although the Communists had attracted several intellectuals and some students had embraced Marxism, few Cubans were willing to accept Communist discipline, which had demanded working agreements with Machado and Batista in the 1930's. The past history of opportunism and political accommodations of the Cuban Communist Party had discredited it in the eyes of the Cuban people and particularly among the students.

By 1950 the Ortodoxos had become a formidable political force. Though lacking a well defined platform, the party's nationalistic program of economic independence, political liberty, social justice, and honest government, and its insistence upon remaining free from political pacts, had won for it a considerable following, especially among University of Havana students. With the slogan "verguenza contra dinero" (honor vs. money) Chibás, now an elected senator, pounded on the consciences of the Cubans in his Sunday radio programs and sought to awaken their minds to the corruption of the Auténtico administrations.[44] Chibás monopolized the rhetoric of revolution, becoming the exponent of the frustrated old generation and the leader of a new generation bent on bringing morality and honesty to Cuban public life. It was he more than anyone else who, with his constant exhortations, calls for reform, and attacks on Cuba's political leadership, paved the way for the revolution that followed.

Many students shared this redemptionist fanaticism, a readiness to sacrifice everything for Cuba's political salvation. In the university, more than anywhere else, the nation's problems were evoked and debated. Theories of all sorts vigorously flourished. The authoritarian ideas of fascism and communism, offering ready formulas to bring order out of Cuba's chaos, were widely discussed. But above all, the nationalistic program of the Ortodoxo Party—economic independence, political liberty, social justice, and an end to corruption—captured the imagination of Cuban youth. Chibás became the idol of university students.

But the hopes of the people were thwarted once more when Chibás, in one of the most bizarre episodes of Cuban political history, shot himself at the end of what started out to be one of his routine weekly radio appeals in August, 1951. Unaware that his radio program was over, Chibás continued speaking. "Cuban people, awake!" were his last words as he pulled a revolver and shot himself in the stomach. Chibás' "last knock on the conscience of the Cubans" and his death several days later produced a feeling of shock and sadness among the emotional masses. His body was taken to the University of Havana, where the Cuban people and the students could mourn him. Chibás' death created a leadership vacuum, produced a rift in the Ortodoxo Party, and facilitated Batista's coup d'etat of March 10, 1952.

A number of reasons have been adduced to explain Chibás' suicide. Some claim that after being unable to prove an allegation of graft he had made against a Prío minister he had no choice but to kill himself. Others blame his suicide on a poll taken before the presidential elections scheduled for 1952. To his surprise the poll showed his popularity waning. Still others point to his unstable personality as the principal cause for him to take his own life. A combination of factors must have no doubt converged on this man's life to provoke such a drastic decision. Foremost among these must have been perhaps the frustration of years of struggle with little apparent results. Despite devoting his life to promoting the ideals of the 1933 revolution, he found that at the end of his long journey he had accomplished little. The evils he had combatted were more prevalent at the time of his death than ever before. Maybe he felt that his death might produce what his life had not—the revolution Martí had envisioned.

By the time of Chibás' death, Cuba's political life was a sad spectacle. Although Prío had introduced a number of reforms, and gangsterism had diminished within the University of Havana campus, his administration resembled that of his predecessor. Politics came to be regarded by the Cuban people with disrespect. To become a politician was to enter into an elite, a new class apart from the interests of the people. The elected politicians did not owe allegiance to their constituents, not even to their nation, but only to themselves and their unsatisfied appetite for power and fortune. Political figures, furthermore, were the object of popular mockery. In particular, the image of the presidency was ridiculed and abused. Chibás' criticism, furthermore, helped to undermine not only the authority of the Auténticos, destroying completely what little prestige they still enjoyed, but the stability of Cuba's political institutions as well.

The breakdown in morale, respect, and values was aggravated by Batista's interruption of constitutional government in 1952. What Cubans believed would never happen again—the return to military rule—became a reality.

4

Insurrection: The Students Against Batista

When on March 10, 1952, General Fulgencio Batista and a group of army conspirators overthrew President Carlos Prío Socarrás' constitutional government, University of Havana students were the first to oppose the new coup d'etat. Students laid their rivalries aside, directing all their efforts against the new regime. Militant anti-Batista student leaders emerged with effective political power not only in the student community but nationally as well. During the first three years of Batista's rule, student opposition was limited to sporadic riots, demonstrations, and protests. Although at the time these unorganized acts may have seemed unimportant, they did help awaken the minds of Cubans to the oppressive nature of Batista's rule and thus paved the way for the insurrection that followed.

THE FEU

Several factors enhanced the importance of University of Havana students during the 1950's. First, the more than 17,000 students attending the University were represented by only one organization, the Federation of University Students (Federación Estudiantil Universitaria or FEU), giving that body concentration and strength. Second, the location of the University in the heart of the capital city exposed the students to the continuous shock waves of Cuba's political turmoil, placing them in an ideal situation for making their political views known. The inadequate student recreational and library facilities and a staff of part-time teachers who lacked a sense of pedagogic responsibility diminished still further the campus' educational atmosphere. Finally, the University's autonomy—originally a sheltering device against government encroachment—had converted it into a sanctuary for political agitators. Because police forces were not allowed to enter the campus, the students had a safe emplacement from which to carry on activities against the government.

Batista was neither popular nor was he accepted as the island's legitimate ruler. The very same day of the coup, and while he was still in the military garrison at Camp Columbia, FEU leaders who for so many years had denounced the Auténtico administration marched to the Presidential Palace to proclaim their support of President Prío and to offer to help him fight the military revolt. Their efforts, however, were in vain. Prío's indecision and the speed with which the conspirators took control of the situation did not allow much action, and the President sought refuge at the Mexican Embassy.[1]

The students returned to their bastion at the University of Havana and from there began to organize demonstrations to repudiate the new regime. The FEU immediately declared a suspension of classes until constitutional guarantees were restored. For several days the students kept a coffin containing the 1940 Constitution on the main steps of the University. When rumors spread that the coffin was to be carried through the streets of Havana in a burial procession, the government tried to talk the students out of it; when unsuccessful, Batista, who knew well what spilling students' blood meant in Cuba, wisely let them go ahead with their plans. After a four-day wake, a procession left the University grounds carrying the casket and took it to the statue of José Martí (Rincón Martiano), where it was solemnly buried. The students claimed in their speeches that they had opposed Prío's regime on the grounds of venality, corruption, and fraud, but that in spite of its weaknesses, it had been a constitutional government. They further declared that the young people of Cuba would never yield to a man like Batista, who took power by a military coup eighty days before democratic elections were to be held.[2]

In a public statement issued soon afterwards, the FEU demanded the restoration of the 1940 Constitution, the reestablishment of civil government, and the holding of free elections. It petitioned Dr. Clemente Inclán, Rector of the University, to dismiss three professors who had accepted jobs in the government. In addition, it claimed that Batista, through his agents, had offered $10,000,000 pesos with which to build the "Ciudad Universitaria," an old dream of the students. "Of course," commented Alejandro Rodríguez Díaz, then member of the FEU, "the offer was rejected and placards were displayed which read 'the university would not surrender and would not let itself be bribed.' "[3]

After this first confrontation with the government, the FEU called on the students to return to classes and continue their campaign against the new ruling group from within the University grounds. On May 20, 1952, a mass meeting took place on the steps of the University to commemorate the establishment of the Cuban Republic. The main speaker of the evening, Jorge Mañach, one of Cuba's most distinguished intellectuals and a former member of the anti-Machado ABC, exhorted the students to carry the banner of opposition against Batista. "I am not an advocate," said Mañach, "of the continuous intervention of students in politics, except at times of great national crisis such as that of the year 1930. Today we are living in one of those times."[4]

Mañach's call found a receptive echo among the students. The students saw themselves as representing the will of the voiceless Cubans. Imitating their predecessors of the generation of 1930, they attempted to assume the traditional and important role of students in national politics. The next month the FEU submitted a "national formula" to solve the political crisis of 1952. The students proposed that Batista resign and that he be replaced by a Provisional President appointed by the Federation to preside until elections were held. Naturally, the government rejected such a plan and responded that the FEU had no authority whatsoever to propose national formulas.[5]

Nonstudent opposition also developed very early. The two major political parties, Ortodoxo and Auténtico, and most of Cuba's politicians opposed Batista through peaceful means, hoping for an honest election. A faction of the Auténticos, however, followers of the deposed President Prío, immediately went underground and began planning a series of insurrectionary activities.

During the first few years of Batista's regime, political parties exerted considerable influence upon the students in Havana. The Ortodoxos were particularly popular and influential among students because of the party's uncompromising attitude toward Batista, the mystique of its martyred leader, Eduardo Chibás, and the fact that its more prominent members included several professors at the University of Havana.

The National Revolutionary Movement, an offshoot of the Ortodoxo party, also commanded strong student support. Led by a University professor, Rafael García Bárcena, this group recruited a number of students for an attack on the military camp that had given Batista command of the army. Bárcena, also a professor at the Escuela Superior de Guerra, a school for army officers, had maintained close contact with the military and expected his attack to coincide with a military coup. Bárcena invited Fidel Castro, who at the time was planning his own Moncada venture, to participate in the attack. But Castro refused. "Fidel thought it was a suicide," explained Angel Díaz, a participant in Castro's Moncada attack. "Besides, Fidel wanted to lead and this one was led by someone else."[6] Batista's intelligence service averted the plot and arrested Bárcena and several fellow conspirators in April, 1953. After brutal police beatings, they were tried and sentenced to prison.[7]

A small faction within the Ortodoxos also advocated violence as the correct tactic to combat Batista. Fidel Castro belonged to this group. After receiving his doctorate of law from the University of Havana in 1950, he joined the party and was nominated as an Ortodoxo candidate to the House of Representatives in the 1952 election. After Batista's coup, he began organizing a small group of followers for his ill-fated attack on the Moncada military barracks in Oriente Province on July 26, 1953.

Castro used the University of Havana as a shelter for his activities. Protected by its autonomy, the campus was a haven for conspirators. Angel Díaz, an attorney and a participant in the Moncada attack, explained that the FEU allowed not only Fidel's but other insurrectionary groups as well to use the University as training grounds. Fidel stored armaments and trained activists within the campus. Yet he was able to recruit only a few students for his venture.[8]

Castro's failure to obtain a large following among students requires some explanation. First, Batista had been in power just a short time and was promising elections and a quick return to constitutional government. His performance in 1944, when he allowed honest elections and permitted Grau to assume the presidency, must have convinced many who would have otherwise followed a violent road to wait a bit longer before resorting to violence. At the time, the population was barely recovering from the shock of the coup, the opposition was divided and powerless, and the army was solidly behind the regime. Violence seemed premature and ill-advised. Second, Castro was not the only one involved in conspiratorial activities within the University. Other groups more influential among the students, such as Bárcenas' had been planning the violent overthrow of Batista's regime. The apparently suicidal nature of Castro's project also failed to convince many students. Finally, Castro was unable to count on the support of his former UIR allies. The professional gunmen in this group refused to accept the leadership of a man of action of lesser stature such as Castro was then.[9]

Castro's attack ended in disaster. Some of the attackers failed even to enter the military barracks. Those who did were massacred by the army. Castro himself escaped to the mountains only to be captured and sentenced to years in prison. The attack had failed. Yet it gave Fidel and his movement national prestige.[10]

Students at the University were influenced particularly by the anti-government stance of several professors. Some members of the faculty were prominent leaders of various political parties. Others, although not identified with any political group, manifested publicly their dissatisfaction with the Batista regime. Time otherwise devoted to classes was consumed in political discussions and in attacks on the Batista regime. Sheltered by the University's autonomy, these professors found in the campus an ideal place for their activities against the government and in the students a receptive audience for their political views.

The government also attempted to influence the students. Batista recognized the "trouble-making" capabilities of the students and tried by two methods to reduce their power. First, he publicly criticized the University's autonomy. In October, 1952, the FEU accused the government of planning to intervene in the University and destroy its autonomy. The University Council, composed of professors and administrative officials, strongly supported the students' accusations.[11]

Realizing the futility of any frontal assault, Batista relied on a second tactic. He attempted to form parallel student organizations to challenge the predominance of the FEU. The first attempt occurred on the occasion of the Eighth Mexican Congress of Architecture, scheduled for August, 1952, in Mexico City, to which the FEU sent a delegation. The government recruited a group of students and provided a military plane for their flight to the Congress. While in Mexico, these students voiced support for Batista. As soon as they returned to Havana, the FEU called an assembly to judge their actions. Amid flying chairs and striking fists, the Federation condemned their behavior. All but three of the twenty-one members of the pro-Batista delegation made public statements supporting the FEU and explaining they had no intention whatsoever of backing the regime.[12]

The government then organized within the University "The First Student Committee for Batista for President." Its purpose was to support Batista's presidential ticket in the approaching national elections, and to run its own candidates in student elections. The FEU opposed this new maneuver and issued a declaration aimed at ending all further government penetration. The statement reminded the students that they were not to engage in any political activity that would contradict the FEU's position against the regime. "Our action is justified," said the Federation, "by the support we have received from the student body." [13] FEU President Alvaro Barba later reaffirmed this stand and added that the mission of the Federation was to coordinate the opposition forces and unite the nation against Batista's usurpation of power.[14]

The relations between Batista and the FEU, which had never been cordial, deteriorated rapidly. Early in 1953, police shot and killed a University of Havana student during a demonstration in front of the school. A national student strike followed. Disorders spread throughout the island; demonstrations against the government occurred almost daily. When the regime announced that the 1953 national elections Batista had promised would be postponed for a year, the FEU quickly accused Batista of perpetuating himself in power. The Federation demanded general elections as soon as possible and a neutral government that could give all parties ample guarantees.[15]

The approaching Worker's Day celebration, traditionally held in Cuba on May 1, offered the students an opportunity to organize a demonstration against Batista. For the 1953 occasion, leaders of the Confederation of Cuban Workers, in agreement with the government, had been preparing a mass meeting to show support for the regime. The FEU invited the leaders of the workers section of the Partido Socialista Popular (Communist) and of the Ortodoxo and Auténtico parties to meet and prepare a gathering parallel to the official meeting. During the organizational discussions, friction arose between the Auténticos and Ortodoxos and the Communists when the latter showed their intention of using the meeting for their own propaganda purposes. In protest against these attempts, the Ortodoxos and Auténticos withdrew their delegation.[16]

By this time several FEU leaders were opposed to the rally and brought pressure upon the Federation's president to call it off. The University Council also appealed to the students and to the Communists not to participate in the event. The Communists finally withdrew their delegation. The FEU, however, went ahead and held the rally at the University stadium with an estimated attendance of 1,000 people. The students, who were the only speakers, attacked the government and censured the Ortodoxo and Auténtico parties for their behavior.[17]

The meeting created much ill feeling within the FEU. Presidents of the student associations of ten facultades issued a public manifesto condemning their fellow members and pointing out that the meeting had produced "a dangerous convergence of the University with Communist elements." Despite such statements others were made justifying the students' action as the product of "passionate feelings." After calm returned to the University, classes, which had been suspended for several days, were resumed.[18]

The May Day celebration afforded another example of a phenomenon often prevalent in Latin American politics—the coming together of the labor and student movements. In Cuba, dissatisfied labor leaders found in their opposition to Batista a common objective with the students. University autonomy offered labor the necessary protection against police action while the traditional political importance of the students increased labor's prestige.

The May Day celebration also brought the Communists and the students together. The Communists aimed at influencing and gaining support among student and labor groups. Unable at this time, due to the international situation, to arrive at a modus vivendi with Batista, the Partido Socialista Popular, Cuba's Communist Party, advocated "a national democratic front government arrived at by the action of the masses." [19] Party Secretary General, Blas Roca, criticized terroristic attempts and other "petit bourgeois" forms of action, labeling them "putschism" and "crazy adventures sometimes hatched out on the University campus." [20]

The mock elections of November, 1954, from which Batista emerged victorious, placed Cuba at a dangerous crossroads. The opposition wanted new elections, while Batista insisted on remaining in power until his new term expired in 1958. Throughout 1955 numerous meetings were held between government officials and oppositionist leaders in an attempt to find a compromise. The failure to reach an agreement forced the Cuban people reluctantly unto a road leading to civil war, chaos, and revolution.

A final attempt to compromise occurred late in 1955 with the emergence of the Sociedad de Amigos de la República (SAR), a nonpartisan organization headed by Colonel Cosme de la Torriente. A distinguished eighty-three-year old jurist and diplomat and a surviving veteran of the Cuban War for Independence, Cosme de la Torriente sought an interview with Batista in which he hoped to influence the government to hold new elections. But Batista refused the interview, alleging Cosme de la Torriente to be simply the leader of another political faction.[21]

Batista's refusal catapulted Cosme de la Torriente into national prominence. Political parties and student leaders rallied to his support. The SAR proposed a public meeting to show mass support for the oppositionist cause and thus perhaps compel the government into allowing new elections.[22]

The rally, one of the largest in Cuba's history, took place in Havana on November 19, 1955, with the participation of most of the opposition political leaders. Recently elected FEU President José A. Echeverría was one of the principal speakers. While he spoke, a group requested that Communist leader Salvador García Agüero be allowed to address the gathering. When their efforts proved futile, they attempted to disrupt the meeting. Fighting broke out. Still on the microphone, Echeverría called for order and asked the crowd "to expel the saboteurs and agents working for Batista." After a brief interruption, during which the Communists were forced to leave, the meeting was resumed.[23]

Sensing the mounting dissatisfaction with his regime and the significance of the SAR's defiance, Batista changed his initial attitude and started lengthy negotiations that came to be known as "El diálogo cívico." These were a series of meetings whereby Cosme de la Torriente, heading a committee of opposition leaders, tried to work out with a similar group of government leaders, a compromise formula. It soon became evident that the Diálogo was doomed to failure. When in March, 1956, Batista's group refused to consider a proposal calling for elections that same year, the negotiations ended.[24]

A new source of controversy was injected into the passionate feeling of the Cubans in 1955 when the regime proposed the construction, with United States support, of a canal through central Cuba. The students once more envisioned their role as representatives of the national will and defenders of the island's sovereignty. The FEU vociferously condemned the idea, calling for a forum at the University of Havana to discuss it. "No man," said Echeverría, "should be allowed to sell our sovereignty and territorial integrity. Our campaign is not against the government, but for the defense of our nationality." When Communist agitators began using the forum to attack the United States and labeled the government a "lackey of Yankee imperialism," Echevarría banned them from the meetings, pointing out that the FEU would not permit the Communists to take advantage of the students' campaign. Aware that the canal idea was producing much opposition, Batistà shelved the plan and feelings subsided.[25]

At the end of 1955, a series of student riots shocked the country. On November 27 the FEU organized a ceremony to honor the memory of eight students shot by Spanish authorities in 1871. When the meeting turned into an anti-Batista rally, police arrested several student leaders, while others had to be hospitalized as a consequence of brutal police methods. Similar events occurred in Santiago, capital of Oriente Province, where police ruthlessly beat students who tried to observe the November 27 commemoration. In protest, the FEU called a student strike which quickly spread throughout the country. All universities, colleges, and secondary schools closed down. For three weeks, daily sorties were made against the police all over the country.

On December 2, students attempting a march from the University of Havana were stopped and beaten by the police. FEU President Echeverría and Vice-President Fructuoso Rodríguez had to be hospitalized. On December 4, during a baseball game, a group of fifteen students ran onto the field displaying banners condemning the regime. Several dozen policemen who had been waiting for the demonstrators surrounded them and beat them brutally in front of thousands of astonished television viewers.[26]

Clashes with the police continued unabated during the following weeks. On December 10, Raúl Cervantes, a popular Ortodoxo youth leader, died from wounds sustained three days earlier in his hometown of Ciego de Ávila, Camagüey Province. Instantly he became a new martyr whose funeral was made into a gigantic symbol of political protest. Thousands attended from all over Cuba, including a delegation from the FEU. Cervantes' death inspired symbolic funerals and more violence. By December 16, Rector Clemente Inclán finally persuaded the Federation to bring the disturbances to a halt. By this time, most student leaders were either in jail or hospitalized. In a final gesture of protest the FEU asked labor and the public to join it on December 14 in a five-minute nationwide work stoppage. The stoppage was widespread despite lack of support from the Batista-oriented hierarchy of Cuban labor.[27]

A month had scarcely gone by when new riots erupted in Havana. The anniversaries of the birth of Martí on January 28 and of the death of a student killed during an anti-Batista demonstration on February 13 were used by the FEU to challenge the government.[28] On February 24 new demonstrations occurred throughout the island to commemorate "El Grito de Baire," which began the War of Independence against Spain in 1895.[29]

On April 19, a group of students attempted to enter a courtroom in Santiago de Cuba to hear the trials of schoolmates accused of participating in riots and illegal possession of arms. Barred from the court, they began demonstrating in the street, dispersing only when fired upon by police and army troops. Two students were wounded fatally, and many were hurt during this encounter. Public indignation in Santiago mounted; retaliations took the lives of two soldiers, one policeman, and two civilians.[30] Most schools throughout Cuba closed, signifying their sympathy with the students of Santiago. Normal school students, attempting to hold a meeting in a public park in the City of Guantánamo, were discouraged by the authorities. Four students were wounded and seven arrested.

Rioting quickly spread to Havana. A group of university students stoned the building of "Televisión Nacional," Channel 4, where a government-sponsored youth program was being televised on April 21. Several participants were wounded. A police cordon was thrown around the grounds of the University of Havana and, on the pretext of searching for hidden arms, government forces entered the University, demolished the Rector's office and destroyed documents, scientific equipment, and furnishings. In one section alone the damage was estimated at $20,000. [31] The action was decried as a violation of university autonomy, and Rector Clemente Inclán suspended classes indefinitely.[32]

Batista replied to the moral indignation of University authorities and students by declaring that the autonomy of the University was limited to educational, administrative, and internal affairs, and that when subversive political elements were entrenched within the University, the government must enforce law and order.[33]

While these riots and demonstrations were going on, other Cubans not connected with student activities were plotting to unseat Batista. Fidel Castro was an early advocate of armed action against the government. After several years in jail following his unsuccessful July 26, 1953, attack on the Moncada barracks, he traveled to the United States and Mexico organizing his 26th of July Movement and seeking followers and funds for the revolutionary cause. In 1956 he vowed to overthrow Batista or to die fighting in the attempt. Another group, known as Montecristi, plotted with army officers to overthrow the regime; Batista uncovered the conspiracy and arrested its principal instigators in April, 1956. That same month another group, belonging to former President Prío's Organización Auténtica, unsuccessfully attacked the Goicuría army barracks in Matanzas Province.[34]

THE DIRECTORIO REVOLUCIONARIO: 1955–1957

Instead of seeking to discourage rebellion by moderation, the regime encouraged it by meeting terrorism with a counter-terrorism that defeated its own ends. By the end of 1955, the leaders of the FEU realized that the efforts of nonpartisan organizations to reconcile government and opposition were futile. They proposed the creation of an insurrectionary movement to lead the struggle for freedom. As the FEU proposal found little response among the electorally-oriented politicians, the students formed their own clandestine organization —the Directorio Revolucionario (Revolutionary Directorate) —in December, 1955. In a secret meeting at the University of Havana on February 24, 1956, Echeverría, as head of the Directorio, announced its creation.[35]

Students themselves were thus assuming the leadership of the anti-Batista struggle. The reason for this bold action requires some explanation. Whereas students from earlier generations had been able to find national leaders embodying their aspirations and ideals, such as Grau or Chibás, these students now were unable to find a comparable charismatic leader. Some of the old leaders of the generation of 1930 seemed to have renounced their early idealism. Others were disillusioned and frustrated. Chibás was dead. National reformist leadership seemed to be either lacking or ineffective. Although the students still identified with some Ortodoxo leaders, they were now unwilling to place their faith too readily on members of the older generation. A generation break stronger perhaps than any other one in Cuban history was taking place in the 1950's—a break that thrusted upon the young the leadership of the anti-Batista movement. The students were still willing to follow a leader, but one from their own ranks. Echeverría thus emerged as the representative of Martí's and Chibás' ideals. He, more than anyone else, commanded the admiration of the students and, as time went by, of the Cuban people.

There were several reasons for organizing a Directorio at this time. One of its founders, Félix Armando Murias, told the author that the students had maintained close contact with labor leaders willing to participate in coordinated actions against the regime. An organization was needed to lead such actions. "Furthermore," said Murias, "members of the FEU who advocated an insurrection against Batista met with opposition within the Federation, adding a note of urgency to the need for a separate organization." [36] In another interview, Armando Fleites, also an active member of the Directorio since its inception and later a commander of the guerrilla forces that fought Batista, explained that during 1955 many labor and professional leaders, disappointed with the electoral negotiations and having no underground movement to which to turn, approached Echeverría to coordinate armed resistance against Batista. Since the Federation operated under the aegis of the University and therefore could not incorporate these nonstudent elements, it was necessary to create an organization outside the FEU that could lead the resistance against Batista.[37]

Out of interviews with former Directorio activists, the following portrait emerges. The student leaders were admirers of Eduardo Chibás and José Martí, sharing the latter's vision of an idealized *patria:* a socially united, racially harmonious, and economically independent country. They were democrats, strongly nationalistic, and anti-Communist. "We opposed agreements with Cuban Communists," said Murias, "whom we considered opportunists and collaborators with Batista since the 1930's." [38]

The students advocated economic reforms: agricultural diversification, industrialization, and agrarian reform. They opposed administrative corruption and other evils of Cuba's public life, and wanted to see the 1940 Constitution fully reestablished and free elections held. Most of them did not aspire to political office, limiting their involvement in politics to the immediate objective of Batista's overthrow, but a few were interested in using student politics as a stepping-stone to national prominence. (After Batista's fall, several Directorio leaders showed their eagerness for positions in the Castro government.) In general, they were well-intentioned but politically unsophisticated young people who desired the best for their country. It is significant to note that several of the FEU and Directorio leaders were from areas other than Havana and many came from poorer or lower middle-class homes. Living away from their families and exposed to the loneliness of a new urban environment, these students stayed close to the campus and were apparently more prone to political involvement than the average city student.

The Directorio differed from other anti-Batista insurrectionary organizations in several ways. First, the Directorio was predominantly a student organization. Not until 1957, after the death of its principal leaders, did nonstudent elements enjoy a degree of importance in the organization and share in the making of its decisions. Second, its leaders believed in tyrannicide and assassination as the means to overthrow the dictatorship. They were, however, strongly opposed to indiscriminate terrorism that might kill innocent people.

The Directorio's plans called for establishing contact with other leaders advocating armed opposition to Batista. One of these, Fidel Castro, had been training an expeditionary force in Mexico and planned to land in Cuba at the end of 1956. Early that year, Echeverría led a student delegation to Mexico, where he signed an agreement with Castro known as "La carta de México" ("The Mexican Letter"). The students pledged a series of diversionary riots in Havana to coincide with Castro's landing on the other end of the island. "Since the landing date had not yet been set," Murias explained, "Castro promised to advise the students as to his exact plans." [39]

A few days after the students returned to Cuba, the Directorio undertook one of its first operations an attempt on the life of Colonel Antonio Blanco Rico, head of Batista's Military Intelligence Service. On October 28, 1956, two members of the Directorio, Rolando Cubela and Juan Pedro Carbó Serviá, fired at Blanco Rico and a group of his friends in a Havana nightclub, killing him and wounding several of his companions. In the ensuing chaos, the attackers escaped. [40]

The assassination brought censure from several sectors of society. Sensing this indignation, Castro told a reporter in Mexico in November, "There was no need to kill Blanco Rico; others deserved to die much more than he did." [41] On the eve of his landing in Cuba, Castro was attempting to project his image to the Cuban people as an advocate of mass struggle against Batista and as opposed to actions of the type perpetrated by the Directorio. He also wanted to discredit the student leaders, whom he considered rivals in the quest for power.

In Oriente Province, a small but well-organized underground force belonging to the 26th of July Movement and led by Frank País, prepared for Castro's arrival set for November 30. On that day commando groups attacked several military installations, touching off a wave of sabotage throughout the province. Terrorism flared, bombs exploded. Underground cells derailed trains and sabotaged power lines, blacking out entire towns.

In Havana, the leaders of the Directorio watched the Oriente developments anxiously, awaiting word from Castro to go into action in the capital. "Fidel's notification," said Murias, "did not come until December 2—the same day he was landing in Oriente." [42] By that time, the uprising had already been crushed and most of the leaders of Castro's 26th of July Movement were either dead or in jail. Batista suspended constitutional guarantees and clamped down total censorship of news. The dreaded military police patrolled the streets of Havana day and night, rounding up suspected revolutionary elements.

Castro's action was supported neither by the general public nor by the regular opposition parties. The army remained loyal to Batista. Castro found refuge in the Sierra Maestra mountains and from there began waging guerrilla warfare against the regime. Lacking word from Castro, afraid the regime might have infiltrated the revolt, and appalled at the speed with which Batista's forces suppressed the uprising, the Directorio leaders in Havana failed to support the Oriente insurgents. [43]

The events in Oriente prompted the University of Havana Council to suspend classes temporarily on November 30, 1956. But as terrorism and violence continued, the Council indefinitely postponed the reopening of the University, which remained closed until early in 1959. [44]

Batista and his clique welcomed the closing of the University. For more than four years the students had been a thorn in their sides. Now the government expected to neutralize student opposition. But the closing of the University instead threw almost 18,000 students into the vortex of national politics. As time went on and the University remained closed, the impatience of the students grew and many began joining insurrectionary organizations. The students narrowed their focus, as their predecessors had in the successful struggle against Machado in the 1930's, to a single, immediate goal: to end the dictatorship.

Despite the instability of the late 1930's, the fall of Machado had ushered in almost two decades of political freedom and constitutional government. The students, and the Cuban people in general, saw Batista's regime as only a temporary interruption of Cuba's democratic political development, as the consequence of Batista's own ambitions for power and Prío's corrupt rule rather than a symptom of more profound national problems. The reduced importance of political institutions at the local level, the reliance on personalismo, the economy's continuing dependence on a single crop, widespread administrative corruption . . . these conditions were not given the recognition they deserved. The elimination of Batista's dictatorship became the panacea to cure all of Cuba's ills. This simplistic thinking served Fidel Castro's purposes well during his stay in the Sierra Maestra, where he proclaimed the overthrow of the regime as the nation's sole, overriding task, avoiding ideological questions as much as possible and advocating only the most obviously popular reforms.

THE DIRECTORIO STRIKES: THE ATTACK ON THE PRESIDENTIAL PALACE

The Directorio planned to overthrow the government by assassinating Batista. The students' leaders reasoned that such a fast and decisive action would cause the regime to crumble and prevent unnecessary loss of life in a possible civil war. Castro blamed Echeverría for the Directorio's inaction at the time of the abortive Oriente uprising. Echeverría apparently felt it was a question of honor to prove both his own courage and the Directorio's determination to fight.[45]

The Directorio was not the only group attempting to kill Batista. Several Auténtico groups followers of former President Prío conspired to unseat Batista and planned an attempt on his life. Led by Daniel Martín Labrandero, a Spanish refugee and former Loyalist officer who had fought against Franco during the Spanish Civil War, one of these groups planned an attack on the Presidential Palace and Batista's assassination. During the summer of 1956 Labrandero recruited a number of discontented elements, including several University of Havana students not connected to the Directorio, for his bold operation. His plans, however, were frustrated when several days before the attack the police discovered and raided the conspirator's headquarters. Labrandero escaped the police's raid only to be arrested several months later. On New Year's Eve, members of his group succeeded in freeing their chief from the Príncipe Prison in Havana, but luck had ran out for Labrandero. Minutes after the escape the police trapped and killed him not too far from the prison walls.[46]

The remainder of Labrandero's group continued to fight. Now led by Carlos Gutiérrez Menoyo, another veteran of the Spanish Civil War and a sergeant in the United States forces in Europe during World War II, they reorganized and made contact with another group led by former Auténtico Congressman Menelao Mora. Mora had his own plans for overthrowing Batista's regime. His knowledge of the palace made him an invaluable asset to the operation. The two groups contacted the Directorio and together they drew plans to storm the palace.[47]

During February, 1957, Herbert L. Matthew's famous interview with Castro took place in the mountains of Oriente Province. On his return trip from the Sierra Maestra, Matthews stopped in Havana and had a secret rendezvous with Echeverría and three other leaders of the Directorio.[48] The students maintained in that meeting that the Directorio had the solid backing of the student body, and that they were awaiting their chance to get into the streets and join a revolution. Echeverría declared that, despite a pact of cooperation he had signed with Castro, students were carrying on parallel but separate operations.[49] "The students told me," wrote Matthews, "they had a plan which would put a definite end to the dictatorship." [50]

The plans of the combined groups called for the storming of the palace and the assassination of Batista. Once the attackers were in control of the palace, they were to assault the Police Headquarters (Cuartel Maestre) and, thereafter, every police station in Havana. The operational headquarters for the revolution was to be established by Echeverría at the University of Havana. From there, arms, supplied mostly by the Auténticos, were to be distributed to the people and operations directed until the final overthrow of the regime.[51]

There were various reasons for the selection of the palace as the site for an attempt on Batista's life. The secrecy surrounding any move of the President outside the palace made it impossible to pinpoint another location for an assassination attempt, and the obvious strong security deployed on such occasions made Batista almost invulnerable. Another reason was perhaps less objective. The plotters felt that by capturing the palace, where the government's vital center was located, they would be able to control the reins of power. Although the plans after the attack were not totally known by those interviewed, it seems that the plotters would have attempted to establish a provisional government, perhaps under the presidency of a distinguished political figure, until elections could be held. One of the individuals considered by the Directorio to head a provisional government was Ortodoxo Senator Pelayo Cuervo Navarro.

Menoyo was named military commander of the attack. Leading fifty men, he was to direct the first attacking wave against the palace and eliminate Batista in his office on the second floor. Directorio leader Faure Chomón was named second in command, and Menelao Mora was appointed civilian commander in charge of nonmilitary operations.[52]

After the first wave had arrived at the palace, a second group, led by Ignacio González, was to surround the palace square and occupy the rooftops of the nearby buildings to hold off army reinforcements. A small group, under the leadership of Calixto Sánchez, was selected to take charge of the airport.[53] A fourth group, led by Echeverría, was to take over "Radio Reloj," CMQ radio station, and broadcast the announcement that the Presidential Palace had fallen and that Batista was dead. Volunteers were to be asked to assemble at the University where they would be given arms and further instructions.[54]

The tentative date for the assault was March 12. At the end of February Menoyo decided that the group needed an operational headquarters. Since money was scarce, the Directorio offered one of its apartments in the Vedado section of Havana. This and other apartments had previously been used by the Directorio as hideouts and for the storage of arms and subversive propaganda. The location proved ideal, and with money donated from the salary of one of the group's members, a second apartment was rented in the same building. On March 9, as the date grew closer, some fifty men moved into the two apartments, arriving a few at a time during the night.[55]

The success of the whole operation depended on the plotter's knowledge of the exact place where Batista was to be at the time of the attack. It was, therefore, necessary that someone who had access to the palace could check on Batista's movements. This task was to be performed by Armando Pérez. Pérez was to telephone the Vedado apartment on March 12 if Batista was in his office. If the call came before three o'clock in the afternoon, the plans for the attack would be put into motion at once. If not, the attack would be postponed until the following day—March 13. [56]

The conspirators remained in the apartment for three days. On March 12 no telephone call came; therefore, the new date was set for the 13. The call came the following morning, shortly after eleven o'clock. Pérez confirmed that the President was in the palace. He planned to have lunch there, and supposedly would be back in his second floor office around three o'clock.[57]

At three o'clock the conspirators left the apartment building and entered three vehicles, two automobiles and a panel truck with the words "Fast Delivery" painted on the sides. Most of them carried machine guns and grenades. All were wearing sport shirts to distinguish them from palace employees and visitors who usually wore jackets and ties.[58]

Less than half an hour after leaving the apartment, the automobile carrying Menoyo and three other men, Luis Goicochea, José Castellanos, and Luis Almeida, reached the Colón Street entrance to the Palace. Without waiting for the two vehicles following, Menoyo stepped out of the car and, firing his submachine gun, killed the four soldiers guarding that entrance. The other three men with him followed at his heels, also firing.[59] The attack caught the palace guards completely by surprise. Batista later said that several members of the guard were at lunch or attending classes inside the palace at the time.[60]

The occupants of the second car, including Chomón and the rest of the attackers in the panel truck, had been cut off from the first car by a passing bus, and were forced to stop several feet away from the palace gate. Leaping out of the truck, the men were met by what Chomón described in his account of the attack as a "shower of bullets." Several of the attackers fled across a nearby park, while others entered the palace.[61]

Of the attackers, only four succeeded in penetrating to Batista's second floor offices, and only one of these survived the revolution to tell about it: Luis Goicochea, a civil administration student. Goicochea was interviewed by CBS correspondent Robert Taber in Cuba after Castro's rise to power. Based on this account, Taber narrates the events of the attack in his book *M–26: Biography of a Revolution*. Part of the narrative that follows is based on that account.

Menoyo, the three men with him, Menelao Mora, and seven

or eight others following closely, ran up to the second floor of the palace looking for Batista. At the top of the stairs, Menoyo and his three companions headed for Batista's offices. A locked door at the end of the hallway barred their progress. One of the men fired his submachine gun at the door's lock, kicking it open. Beyond them was a kitchen and a dining room with three frightened servants who were pushed into a corner. The attendants said that the President had just taken his after-luncheon coffee and had retired. They did not know where he had gone. They were searched for weapons and left unharmed.[62]

Menoyo and his three companions headed for Batista's offices. The conspirators had been provided with a detailed floor map of the palace indicating a secret passage leading from Batista's offices to his residential quarters on the floor above. They could not find any such passage. Their attempt, furthermore, to reach the third floor seemed almost impossible. Machine gun and rifle fire was coming from the third floor; the troops there were directing their aim at anything that moved. The conspirators had little ammunition left, and the sound of shooting above warned them that their time was running short.[63]

In the meantime, Batista reinforcements began to arrive. The second group that was supposed to prevent this failed to appear. A group of sailors sent from the nearby Navy Department arrived in the vicinity and began advancing toward the palace. Also, army units were dispatched toward the area from Camp Columbia.[64]

The four men that had entered the presidential suite decided to withdraw. Three more, Juan Pedro Carbó Serviá, José Machado, and José Luis Gómez Wangüemert, were now added to the group. While descending to the ground floor, Castellanos was killed by machine gun fire from the upper floor; Menoyo, infuriated, leaped into the open, and he, too, was instantly hit. The remaining five were able to make it safely to the street door they had used to enter the building.[65]

In the street lay the bodies of eight or ten youths who had died trying to reach the palace. Wangüemert was the first to make the inevitable decision to run across the street and into the park. He had gone only a few steps when he was hit by machine gunners in the palace. Carbó Serviá and Machado followed. Goicochea, too, started across the street. He heard a shout behind him and, turning his head as the guns above started again to shoot, saw Almeida still at the palace entrance —the last time he was to see him alive.[66]

The three were able to escape. Goicochea hid in an apartment in the Vedado section of Havana, while Carbó Serviá and Machado found refuge in an apartment in Humboldt 7, also in the Vedado area. Chomón, wounded and bleeding, had previously escaped through another door.

Despite the audacity of the assault, the strong palace defense had held out. The poor quality of the attackers' weapons and the failure of reinforcements to arrive turned possible victory into costly defeat. According to the official government report, twenty were killed, including five members of the palace guard. That figure, however, did not include the many conspirators who were hunted down and killed by the police after the event.

While the palace attack was going on, another group, led by Echeverría, stormed a Havana radio station. Unaware of the failure at the palace, the students broadcasted an announcement that Batista had been killed and his regime brought down. The students' joy was short-lived. In an encounter with government forces minutes later, the police shot and killed Echeverría and wounded several other students.[67]

STUDENTS, COMMUNISTS, AND CASTRO: 1957–1958

Fidel Castro, from his hideout in the mountains, criticized the students' attack. In a taped interview shown in the United

States in May, Castro called it "a useless waste of blood. The life of the dictator is of no importance . . . Here in the Sierra Maestra is where to fight." [68] Throughout his stay in the mountains, Castro opposed a military coup, the assassination of Batista, or any other violent act by any group not directly under the control of his 26th of July Movement.

Another group that spoke against the attack on the Presidential Palace, and against Castro's landing in Oriente as well, was the Partido Socialista Popular (PSP), Cuba's Communist party. The head of the PSP, Juan Marinello, wrote to Herbert L. Matthews on March 17, 1957, explaining the official party line: "In these days, and with reference to the assaults on barracks and expeditions from abroad—taking place without relying on popular support—our position is very clear: we are against these methods." The Communists advocated, as the correct strategy against Batista, a mass struggle based primarily on the mobilization of the proletariat and leading toward national elections. They called for the creation of a Democratic Front of National Liberation to form a government representing the workers, peasants, urban petty bourgeoisie, and national bourgeoisie, all under the leadership of the proletariat.[69]

But the PSP leaders were following a dual strategy. While publicly advocating peaceful opposition to Batista, they were secretly making overtures to the insurrectionary groups for closer collaboration. As early as December 1955, Raúl Valdés Vivó, Secretary-General of the Juventud Socialista, the youth branch of the PSP, held meetings with Directorio leaders Echeverría and Fructuoso Rodríguez, pressing for closer relations with their organization. Vivó also advocated a "united front" of all students, including the Directorio but under the leadership of the FEU.[70] The Communists, encouraged by their success in electing Amparo Chaple, a member of the Juventud, to the presidency of the student's association of the School of Philosophy at the University of Havana in November, 1955, apparently believed they could eventually dominate the FEU and neutralize the Directorio by placing the latter under the

Federation's control. But no union emerged out of these early Communist contacts with the students. Echeverría and other student leaders were not ready for an alliance with the Communists and went ahead with their plans for the Directorio.[71]

Throughout most of Batista's rule, the Communists had enjoyed virtually complete liberty; several of them even held minor posts in the government. Batista took certain measures against the PSP, principally to appease the United States government. These were few, however, compared to the persecution suffered by the non-Communist opposition. The PSP, directly and through its University Bureau at the University of Havana, consistently sought to undermine, infiltrate, and control the groups combating Batista. The importance of the Directorio as a dangerous rival for power, and the militant anti-Communism of several of its leaders were constantly present in the minds of the top members of the PSP.

The defeat suffered at the palace was further aggravated by the assassination a month later of four of the Directorio's remaining top leaders. On April 20, 1957, police surrounded an apartment building on Humboldt Street in Havana and massacred acting FEU President Fructuoso Rodríguez, Joe Westbrook, Juan Pedro Carbó Serviá, and José Machado.[72] That the police had been able to locate the students' hideout without help seemed almost impossible to the friends and family of the murdered youths. Every indication pointed toward a police informer among the students. An investigation, however, would have to await Batista's downfall.[73]

Following the "Humboldt events," as this episode was later known, there were several student demonstrations, mostly by high school students. These, however, soon died out as police repression increased. Considering it unwise to resume classes, the University Council kept the University closed. Almost totally inactive, the FEU held a meeting to select a new president but abstained from issuing any political statement. With the death of Rodríguez, successor of Echeverría to the FEU presidency, and the asylum in the Mexican Embassy of Juan Nuiry, next in line, Amparo Chaple became the first woman president of the organization. Her reign, however, was short-lived. Her Communist leanings and the fact that she had visited Czechoslovakia shortly before prompted the Federation to oust her and to vote Miguel Ramón Prendes as president.[74]

The "Humboldt events," the failure of the attack on the Presidential Palace, and the death of Echeverría, at the time perhaps the most popular figure opposing Batista, left the Directorio leaderless and disorganized. Almost a year went by before the organization recovered from the blow, and even then it never regained the prestige and importance it had enjoyed prior to the palace assault. While the Directorio declined, Castro, unchallenged in the mountains, grew in prestige, strength, and following. He gained adherents in the cities and won over many discontented elements who, whatever differences with his 26th of July Movement they might have had, found no other insurrectionary organization to join.

The remaining Directorio leaders went into exile and began reorganizing under the direction of Faure Chomón. In a speech in Miami, on October 20, 1957, Chomón advocated unity among the revolutionary groups, called for "a nationalistic united party of the Revolution," and condemned the United States for selling arms to Batista.[75] Chomón also supported the unity efforts of representatives from seven anti-Batista organizations, including the Directorio and the 26th of July Movement, who had gathered in Miami following Castro's July, 1957, "Manifesto of the Sierra Maestra" calling for a united front to overthrow Batista. Out of that meeting, a unity pact was signed on November 1, 1957, and a Cuban Liberation Council (Junta de Liberación Cubana) organized.[76]

The Junta, however, was short-lived. In a letter sent to its members on December 14, 1957, Castro explained that he opposed the Miami unity pact because it failed "to reject foreign [U.S.] intervention in Cuba's internal affairs and to repudiate a military junta after Batista's downfall." Castro wrote further that the Junta's pretensions "to approve or disapprove of the provisional president's appointment of cabinet members and to incorporate all revolutionary forces into the armed forces after victory" were unacceptable. "The 26th of July Movement," asserted Fidel, "claims for itself the functions of directing the revolutionary struggle and of reorganizing the armed forces of the nation." [77] After Batista's overthrow, Castro disclosed that he had withdrawn from the Junta because he realized he was not strong enough to dominate the other groups in a single front.[78]

Following the murder of the 26th of July Movement's underground leader, Frank País, by Batista's police on July 30, 1957, a spontaneous strike broke out in the three easternmost provinces of Cuba. This strengthened Castro's conviction that a general strike could topple the regime. The 26th of July Movement did finally organize a general strike on April 9, 1958, but it failed, setting off an ideological struggle within the Movement. The main subject of controversy was apparently the problems of relations with the Communists. Although the PSP had sent representatives to the Sierra prior to the April 9 strike, apparently no formal agreement had been reached with Fidel. The Communists failed to support the strike blaming its failure on the 26th of July Movement's "unilateral call, without counting on the rest of the opposition or on the workers themselves." [79]

Meanwhile, the Directorio leaders prepared to resume their struggle against Batista. Instead of the traditional tactic of fighting in urban areas, the students now decided to establish a guerrilla focus in the island. Several reasons can be advanced for this tactical shift. First, underground activities in the cities were by this time extremely risky. Repression had increased. Fear of Batista's police discouraged many who otherwise would have been willing to hide and help underground fighters. Then Castro's success in the mountains encouraged similar attempts. By opening a guerrilla front in the center of the island, the students felt they would be closer to the capital than the other guerrilla forces and could control Havana, which was considered to be the key to capturing power. Finally, some of the Directorio leaders were nonstudents and did not share in the traditional attachment of students to urban actions.

Early in 1958, a Directorio force sailed from Miami, landed in Cuba, and started guerrilla activities in the mountains of central Cuba. But differences arose within the Directorio in the mountains. One group, commanded by Faure Chomón and claiming that the correct strategy was *golpear arriba* (strike at the top), advocated moving back to Havana to reorganize the Directorio underground and assassinate Batista. Another, led by Eloy Gutiérrez Menoyo and Armando Fleites, urged a continuation of guerrilla warfare. Menoyo and Chomón also clashed over who should direct the military operations and over Chomón's decision to send a quantity of badly needed weapons to Havana.

In mid-1958 the two factions finally split. Fleites told the writer that his group, later known as the "Second Front of the Escambray," continued to fight Batista as an independent organization opposing alliances with the 26th of July Movement or any other group. Toward the end of 1958, he said, his force numbered about 1,000 men, mostly farmers and residents of the area.[80]

Of the remaining members of the Directorio, some, led by Chomón, returned to Havana and began rebuilding the underground, while others, commanded by Rolando Cubela, carried on small guerrilla operations in the mountains. Responding to Castro's invitation to new unity talks, the Directorio sent delegates to the Sierra Maestra in mid-1958. In July, representatives for several anti-Batista organizations, excluding the PSP, met in Venezuela and signed a new unity pact known as the "Caracas Letter." [81] The Communists were excluded from the Caracas meeting because of the opposition of several groups represented there. Castro, however, was holding parallel talks with PSP leaders at the time.[82] Meantime, in Havana, Chomón and his small student underground faced mounting repression. Finally the students went back to the mountains. There the Directorio allied itself with 26th of July Movement forces under Che Guevara, three months before Batista's regime collapsed.[83]

5
Castro
and the Students

The crumbling of Batista's regime on January 1, 1959, marked a turning point in the history of Cuba's student movement. Advocating unity among the revolutionary forces that had fought Batista and claiming that State and University were now identical, Castro proceeded to seize control of the student movement and the University of Havana, expelling dissident students and professors.

How was this accomplished? Of the several groups that had fought Batista, the 26th of July Movement had an almost undisputed claim to fill the vacuum left by the dictator. Castro's charisma and his revolutionary prestige made him in the eyes of the Cuban people the logical occupant of Batista's vacant chair; he was the man of the hour, the new messiah. The other insurrectionary organizations lacked the mystique, the widespread support, and the organized cadres of Castro's movement. The Second Front of the Escambray was a localized guerrilla group without much following in the cities. The Civic Resistance Movement, formed by prominent professionals and university professors, was an amorphous group that followed Castro's orientations. The PSP had accepted Castro's leadership and seemed willing to cooperate with the "petty bourgeois" revolutionary. Most politicians had lost prestige by participating in Batista's rigged elections of November, 1958. Furthermore, the regular army, which might otherwise have been able to take over, was leaderless and demoralized. Castro's bid for power seemed unchallenged.

The Directorio Revolucionario, however, had a chance to confront the national hero from a position of strength. Prior to Castro's triumphant arrival in Havana, the Directorio underground, led by Faure Chomón, occupied key positions in the city, including the Presidential Palace and the University of Havana. The students also took large quantities of weapons from a military base near the capital and moved them to the University. "Some Directorio leaders, and especially Chomón," said Directorio activist Jorge Nóbrega later, "wanted an active role in the new government." [1] Angered because a provisional government had already been formed in Santiago de Cuba without its participation, the Directorio demanded that other insurrectionary organizations also share power. "The victory belongs to all," emphasized Chomón at the time, "and none should try to impose his will." [2]

As soon as he arrived in Havana, Castro demonstrated his tactical ability by outmaneuvering his young rivals. In his first victory speech, he pleaded with the students' mothers to take their weapons away. "Arms for what?" asked Castro. "The time to fight is over. What we now need is unity." [3] In a televised appearance the next day, he criticized the Directorio leaders, particularly Chomón.[4] Portraying the students as ambitious divisionists, he was able to turn public opinion against them. Faced with mounting pressure, the Directorio had no choice but to end its defiance and turn over its strongholds to the 26th of July Movement.

Castro immediately rewarded those willing to support him. Former Directorio leader Major Rolando Cubela was appointed military attaché to the Cuban Embassy in Spain and later Under-Secretary of the Ministry of the Interior. José Naranjo, who had worked closely with the 26th of July Movement while Directorio coordinator in the United States in 1958, was appointed Minister of Interior. Although remaining outside the government in 1959, Chomón decided to support Castro's move to the left and endorsed the ensuing purge of anti-Communist elements within the revolution.[5] Castro rewarded Chomón with an ambassadorship to the Soviet Union in 1960 and later with a cabinet post. A host of minor governmental positions went to less prominent Directorio members. Some students, however, were alienated by Castro's accelerating shift leftward; others quietly resumed their studies.

The University of Havana reopened its doors early in 1959. Old student leaders and new ones, emerging out of the insurrectionary struggle, took provisional charge of the FEU. They saw as their first task the transformation of an archaic university into an academically modern, politically progressive institution. To that end, students and faculty formed a University Reform Commission. The Commission immediately organized revolutionary tribunals to purge professors, students, and employees who had collaborated with Batista. Once the alma mater had been "purified," the Commission drew plans to reform the University's structure and curriculum and called for student elections in October to renew the FEU's leadership.[6]

The approaching elections prompted the government to intervene. To mobilize and indoctrinate the students, control of the FEU was essential. Castro advocated unity among the various student factions and urged the "election" of one candidate by acclamation. In a meeting held with Rolando Cubela and Pedro L. Boitel—the two candidates for president of FEU —and with other students, Castro's brother, Raúl, backed Cubela.[7]

There were several reasons for this choice. Cubela worked with the government and supported the Castro brothers. Although he was not directly involved in student affairs, he enjoyed great popularity at the University. The Castro brothers may also have seen in Cubela certain personality weaknesses to be exploited to their own advantage.[8] Finally, the alternative to Cubela, Pedro Boitel, opposed and was opposed by the

Communists.[9] To ensure complete control, Raúl placed three unconditional Castro supporters as Cubela's running mates: Major Angel Quevedo, Ricardo Alarcón, and José Rebellón.

As the election approached, government pressure increased. The day before the voting, Fidel asked Boitel to withdraw his candidacy.[10] The next morning, October 17, 1959, the official government newspaper *Revolución* carried on its front page Castro's exhortation to the students to unite and name the FEU president by acclamation rather than by election. "All students," the paper quoted Fidel, "should proclaim one president unanimously. That will really be a victory for all and not the Pyrrhic triumph of one group." Then Raúl Castro, to leave no doubt where the government's support lay, accompanied Cubela to the University and spoke to the students on Cubela's behalf. In addition, Minister of Education Armando Hart met with the two candidates and asked Boitel to withdraw from the race.[11]

Under these pressures, Boitel called a student assembly and offered not to run. But the students demanded an election. Their insistence should not be interpreted so much as a rebuke of Fidel, but rather as part of the student political tradition at the University of Havana, where elections had been held every year prior to 1956.

The revolutionary regime enjoyed the support of a great majority of the students and, for that matter, of the Cuban people. The students were largely unaware of the pressures and maneuvers going on behind the scenes. Many, reading Castro's appeal in the newspapers on the morning of the election and hearing rumors that Boitel had withdrawn his candidacy, expected no elections and stayed away from the polls. With approximately half of the student body voting, Cubela won the elections. He received 52 percent of the votes to Boitel's 48 percent.[12] There were no other elections until 1962, when José Rebellón was "elected" president of the FEU. He was the sole candidate. Pedro L. Boitel had been sentenced to forty-two years in prison in 1960 for "counterrevolutionary activities."

"Elections" were held again on February 10, 1965. Jaime Crombet became the new FEU president, the students having cast their votes for a single preselected list of candidates presented at a general assembly of the entire student body. In January, 1966, the regime reshuffled the leadership of the Federation, replacing Crombet with Francisco Dorticós as president. This *fait accompli* was later "publicly approved" by an assembly of the student body.[13] In an attempt to raise the Federation prestige, the regime allowed elections in December, 1966. [14] The two candidates, however, were members of the Union of Young Communists (Unión de Jóvenes Comunistas or UJC), the youth branch of Cuba's Communist Party.

Cubela's election gave Fidel Castro only partial control of the University. Its autonomy still sheltered the campus from further interference; the University Council could still decide internal matters. Castro's desire to direct the university reform movement became the issue over which State and University clashed. Autonomy was the obstacle—control the prize.

An early attempt to subvert the University's autonomy occurred simultaneously with the FEU election campaign in 1959. On October 7, Professor Raúl Roa, Minister of Foreign Relations proposed that the University Council ask the government to appoint several cabinet members to form a joint committee with the deans of the faculties to plan university reform. The Council, pretending that this proposal was not contrary to university autonomy, adopted Roa's proposal and petitioned the government accordingly.[15] The uproar this request produced among teachers and students and the regime's stake in the approaching student elections, however, convinced the government that the time was not yet ripe for such a move. Castro shelved the Council's petition.

A second assault on the University's autonomy occurred in 1960. At a time when the government's power was expanding into every sector of Cuban society, the University still enjoyed relative independence. Arguing that autonomy had special significance when State and University clashed, but was anachronistic when they coincided, Castro's Cabinet proposed to participate in planning university reform and sent representatives to explain this view to the student-faculty University Reform Commission established early in 1959. The government demanded a role for the Ministries of Education and Finance and the National Institute of Agrarian Reform in shaping university policy.[16] But this threatened intervention again met with the professors' stern opposition.

The government then made a final attempt, this time through the Student Federation. In a joint declaration issued in April, 1960, the federations of the universities of Havana, Las Villas, and Oriente requested the creation of a "Higher Council" composed of government representatives, faculty members, and students from the three state colleges to coordinate Cuba's university education. Although opposing this new attempt, the University Council did agree that two students and two faculty members from each university should form a committee—without government representation—to coordinate reform plans.[17]

Despite this concession, the University Council remained in control. But the government-controlled FEU refused to cooperate and the new committee soon died out. Meanwhile, the 1959 University Reform Commission had lapsed into inactivity. The Federation needed an incident to justify the government's complete intervention in university life. This occurred in mid-1960. The crisis was provoked after the University Council refused to approve the actions of several engineering students led by José Rebellón, who accused two professors of being "counterrevolutionary," ejected them from the University of Havana, barred them from their classrooms, and—without any legal authority—advertised in the press for replacements.[18] The Council sided with the two professors while the FEU, although it apparently had not been formally involved in the "expulsion," supported Rebellón's action.

Verbal attacks and counterattacks followed. Castro's official press began a defamatory campaign against the Council. Charging that "reactionary" professors were attempting to provoke a crisis to damage the revolution, the FEU demanded the Council's resignation. Several professors resigned. Pro-Castro students occupied University buildings. Finally, on July 15, a group of about fifty professors and the leadership of the FEU organized a new revolutionary council. The professors who refused to accept the new junta were expelled, forced to resign, or pensioned off. The government soon sanctioned this university coup and at the request of the new council passed legislation legalizing its functions. Nearly eighty percent of the old faculty members were replaced with professors favorable to the revolution.[19] The regime dealt a final blow to university autonomy on December 31, 1960, when it created a Higher Council of Universities, patterned after the "Higher Council" proposed by the students in April and headed by the Minister of Education, to rule the three state universities.[20]

The students' coup converted the autonomous University of Havana into an extension of the State. Credit for this transformation must also be given to Carlos Rafael Rodríguez, one of the PSP's top theoreticians. In March, 1960, Rodríguez became Professor of Political Economy at the University. Working together with Héctor Garcini—a law professor and legal adviser to Cuba's President, Osvaldo Dorticós—and with FEU leaders, Rodríguez helped plan the take-over. Minister of Education Armando Hart and two student leaders, Ricardo Alarcón and Isidoro Malmierca, also played a key role in the July crisis.[21]

Rodríguez remained in the background, allowing others to occupy important positions. By the end of 1961, however, he became the University's representative on the Higher Council of Universities and the guiding force behind plans for reform.[22] At the time of the July events, Rodríguez explained to a reporter, the Communists' tactic had been "thorough cooperation with Castro." The government and the PSP had agreed that non-Communists as well as Communists could teach at the University, but that the institution would have to be dedicated "to the complete service of the revolution." [23] Having fulfilled his mission at the University of Havana, Rodríguez moved, in February, 1962, to the presidency of the National Institute of Agrarian Reform. In January of that same year the president of the PSP, Juan Marinello, became rector of the University.[24]

STUDENTS AGAINST CASTRO:
THE OPPOSITION FAILS

Although it is difficult to specify student attitudes under Castro with any precision, at least three general orientations can be distinguished during the first year and a half of Castro's rule.

One group of students supported both the revolution and its shift to the left. Some of these students backed Fidel faithfully, but—in keeping with the Latin American tradition of personalismo—followed the man rather than his ideas. Others in this group supported Castro's policies: his stand vis-à-vis the United States, his implementation of economic and social reforms, and his insistence on ending administrative corruption. Many of these pro-Castro students were caught up in the mystique of revolution, eager to do whatever was necessary to help the government. The regime, furthermore, fostered the students' feeling of participation by increasing their opportunity to join in the revolutionary process. Still others, coming from lower income families, found that by aligning themselves with the revolution they could better their social status and strike at more privileged students. A common characteristic of all the students in this first group was their identification with the "fatherland" more than with specific ideology, such as Marxism. The group included, however, a small but militant and disciplined Marxist-Leninist element which usually followed PSP directives and which strongly influenced other pro-Castro students.

A second group, quite small, opposed the revolution. Its

ranks were filled mostly with students whose families had been adversely affected by Castro's reforms.

A third group of students favored the revolution but opposed Communist influence in the government. Their opposition had varied origins. Some of those who had participated actively in the anti-Batista struggle abhorred Castro's purges of revolutionary figures.[25] Others resented the rapid and often chaotic changes brought on by Castro's reforms. Many feared the regime's absolutist tendencies and its intervention in university affairs. But overriding all these views was a fourth orientation, shared by virtually all these students during this early period: a willingness to justify government excesses as the natural result of transitional times.

Student opposition to the Castro regime was at first amorphous, but as the tempo of the revolution increased and the Communists gained in strength, it took on definite form. Late in 1959 and throughout 1960, anti-Castro organizations established branches within the University of Havana.[26] Among them, one known as Trinchera (The Trench), whose leaders originated from the Catholic University Association (Agrupación Católica Universitaria), soon acquired some importance. The Church provided the framework for these students' anti-Communist activities, offering them a doctrinal alternative to communism. Through their newspaper, *Trinchera,* they were among the first to denounce Communist gains within the revolution. One of their leaders, Juan Manuel Salvat, told the author that throughout 1959 *Trinchera* supported the revolution but, aware of the struggle between Communists and non-Communists within the government, was committed to fight to prevent the Communists from taking control.[27]

The Trinchera group sought to alert the Cuban people to the Communist challenge mainly through protests, riots, and propaganda. In February, 1960, they demonstrated against Soviet Vice-Premier Anastas Mikoyan's visit to Havana. Minutes after Mikoyan had placed a wreath on the statue of José Martí in the city's Central Park, the students attempted a similar ceremony to show their discontent. Police fired shots into the air and arrested twenty students. The following month, while Trinchera students marched from the University in support of Luis Conte Agüero, a popular radio and television commentator then waging an anti-Communist campaign, FEU leaders and student militias recently organized by the FEU gave them a brutal beating.[28]

Soon after these events, seeking to organize and lead an active struggle against the regime, the Trinchera group joined the Revolutionary Recovery Movement (MRR). The MRR's origins dated back to the insurrectionary era, when it was called the Legion of Revolutionary Action. One of its military leaders, Manuel Artime, had fought briefly against Batista in the mountains and had later worked with the revolutionary government. After breaking with Castro, he and other rebel army officers organized the MRR. Several student leaders had belonged to and kept in close contact with Artime's organization; after the anti-Mikoyan demonstration, they formed the Revolutionary Student Directorate (Directorio Revolucionario Estudiantil or DRE) of the MRR within the University of Havana and tried to build a student underground.[29]

The activities of the DRE and other anti-Castro groups interfered with the government's attempts to control the University. Castro and the controlling group within the FEU recognized the danger and acted accordingly. The Federation set up disciplinary tribunals to judge and expel "counterrevolutionary" students and suspended some of its own officials who had been involved in the anti-Mikoyan demonstration. FEU President Cubela called for the expulsion of "the traitors who conspired against the University." [30] Students burned bundles of *Trinchera* and other anti-Communist propaganda. Dissenters, including DRE leaders Alberto Müller and Juan Manuel Salvat, were beaten, threatened, and bodily forced off the campus.

At the same time, Raúl Castro inaugurated a new scholarship plan through his Ministry of Defense to expand opportunities in higher education for the children of workers and peasants.[31] In the process, support for the regime from these less privileged social sectors naturally increased. By implementing this plan, the government was able to swell university enrollments with loyal followers and effectively stifle student opposition.

Denied the shelter of the University, the DRE leaders had to choose between the underground, imprisonment, or exile. In mid-1960, after several months in the underground, Müller and Salvat escaped to the United States. In Miami the DRE broke with the MRR and joined the Democratic Revolutionary Front, a loosely coordinated body of anti-Castro organizations. The close relations that existed between the MRR and the students continued. Artime explained that a separate organization made the students happy, while at the same time it could still be influenced by the MRR and would provide the two groups with greater power within the Front.[32] Shortly thereafter, the two students, together with several others, returned clandestinely to Cuba to organize resistance in schools and universities.[33]

As a group, the DRE students were an interesting lot. Most came from middle- and upper-class families, usually professionals and businessmen. Some were active in Catholic youth organizations. The Church's influence on them was strong, although decreasingly so over time. A few came from areas outside of Havana, but most were from the capital. They were young, usually in their early twenties. Some belonged to the old anti-Batista generation; others had entered the university after Castro came to power. Like their predecessors in the Directorio, these students were well-intentioned and courageous, but lacked political maturity. Beyond the overthrow of Castro, they had no clear goals. Recognizing the United States government as the world's most powerful anti-Communist force, they sought and welcomed its help. "We expect aid and weapons from our neighbors to the north and will always be grateful [to them]," wrote Müller in January, 1961, "but we will never be servants or vassals." [34]

The ideas of the DRE leaders were within the mainstream

of Cuba's political thought. The students shared Martí's vision of an ideal *patria,* friendly to but not dependent upon the United States. They had supported the program of nationalism, social justice, and political democracy expounded by Castro in the early days of his regime. When it became evident, however, that the revolution was moving toward communism, they joined the anti-Castro ranks.

The DRE leaders adhered to Christian ideals. They felt their task was to warn the Cuban people of the materialistic, atheistic nature of communism. In an editorial in *Trinchera,* they claimed the Communists denied "human freedom, property rights, freedom of thought, and family, love, and religion" and accused the PSP of "treachery to the spiritual values of Martí's fatherland." "While the Communists are materialists," they wrote, "the Cuban people and students are humanists." After the hoped-for overthrow of the Castro regime, the DRE advocated a "national Christian order based on freedom and justice and a youth movement based on Christian principles and ideals.[35]

The DRE never attained the prominence of the anti-Batista Directorio. There are several reasons for this. While the Directorio was organized after nearly four years of Batista's rule, when opposition was widespread, the DRE was formed when Castro still enjoyed a great deal of support. Furthermore, the DRE had a limited base of support; unlike the Directorio, it worked exclusively among students. Finally, the DRE lacked a leader comparable in popularity to José Antonio Echeverría. Even had they had such a figure, it is doubtful that the anti-Castro Cubans would have been ready to place their complete faith in one man, disillusioned as they were with the *personalista* tradition Castro had so effectively appropriated. The unwillingness of many anti-Castro Cubans to accept any strong, charismatic leader is perhaps an important reason why they remain disunited to this day.

By the summer of 1960, Porfirio Remberto Ramírez—a student leader closely connected with the DRE, who had fought

against Batista and after Castro's victory had been elected
President of the FEU at the "Marta Abreu" University in Las
Villas Province—was completely disenchanted with Castro
and with the mounting Communist influence in his movement.
Ramírez took up arms again, hoping to open a guerrilla front
in the mountains of central Cuba. A Castro firing squad ended
his brave guesture on October 13, 1960. [36]

In the months that followed Ramírez' execution, the activities of the DRE and the anti-Castro underground reached
their high-water mark. When Fidel spoke at the University of
Havana on November 30, several bomb explosions reaffirmed
the DRE's determination to end his regime. In January, 1961,
the DRE sabotaged Havana's electric power plant, and in February, on the first anniversary of the anti-Mikoyan demonstration, it organized a partially successful national student strike.
In April, 1961, a small group led by Alberto Müller began
guerrilla activities in Oriente Province.

Also in April the DRE was to participate in a coordinated
plan to assassinate Castro and capture Havana. Men and
weapons had been requested from exile organizations for this
so-called "April 9 Plan." Its leaders had no program other than
the establishment of a provisional government. Manuel Ray's
Revolutionary Movement of the People (MRP) had been
given the task of assassinating Castro. The DRE shared the
MRP's view that the underground forces were indispensable
to success in overthrowing Castro's government. The two
groups saw the landing of the United States-sponsored Cuban
invasion force, then being trained by the CIA in Guatemala,
as the culminating event to follow a series of uprisings and acts
of sabotage they hoped would split Castro's army throughout
the island and weaken the regime's hold over the people.[37]

The plan was doomed to fail. The planners in exile disre-
garded the underground forces in Cuba and placed an unjusti-
fied faith in the invasion's success. Arms that were to be
shipped to DRE forces in the mountains never arrived and
communications between the exile and underground forces

were sporadic and confused. "The lack of support from the groups in exile," DRE leader Fernández Rocha later complained bitterly, "and their failure to supply badly needed war matériel, frustrated the 'April 9 Plan' in its early stages." Rocha claimed further that "the underground was not advised at all of the invasion plans. Not until April 17, the very day of the landing, did we receive word that the invasion had been launched." [38] The DRE inside Cuba watched the Bay of Pigs disaster in confusion and frustration.

The failure of the invasion and the brutal repression that followed smashed the entire Cuban underground. On the first day of the invasion the regime arrested thousands of real and suspected oppositionists. The resistance never recovered from the blow. Müller was captured by Castro's army, tried, and sentenced to twenty years in prison. Of the other DRE leaders, many were apprehended—a few were executed—and many went into exile.[39]

After a short stay in Miami, a small DRE force led by Fernández Rocha was smuggled into Havana to begin rebuilding the underground. But early in 1962 the DRE was infiltrated by Jorge Medina Bringuier, a captain in Castro's intelligence service. Taking advantage of his friendship with several students, Medina posed as an anti-Castroite and attained an important position within the remnants of the DRE's Havana underground.[40] The final blow fell in mid-1962, in an operation planned and directed by Raúl Castro. Most of the remaining DRE members were arrested. A few were purposefully not captured in hopes they would in turn reorganize and expose others.[41]

CASTRO IN CONTROL:
MOBILIZATION AND PURIFICATION

Castro had promoted loyal Fidelistas as FEU presidents, ended university autonomy, purged dissenting students and professors, and destroyed the DRE. But he still needed a centralized body that could control Cuba's youth and insure their loyalty to his regime. Early in 1960, Castro established the Association of Young Rebels (AJR), the equivalent of the Soviet Komsomol. In October, the youth branches of the 26th of July Movement, the PSP and the Directorio (the latter still under Chomón's leadership) merged into the new association.[42] Over the next two years, the AJR expanded until it controlled every youth group in Cuba. In the case of the FEU of the University of Havana, however, a special arrangement was made. While it, too, merged with the AJR, the FEU maintained its existing structure and leadership. In 1962 the Association of Young Rebels changed its name to the Union of Young Communists (UJC), and organized a University Bureau in charge of political indoctrination within the University of Havana.[43]

Two reasons can be advanced for the special treatment given the FEU. First, the Federation's prestige abroad enabled Castro to influence international student movement and congresses and provided an ideal vehicle for the penetration of Latin American universities. Second, the dissolution of the FEU would have alienated many students who still revered the organization's tradition and past importance.

By 1967 the government felt it unnecessary to preserve the University Bureau of the UJC and the FEU as two distinct organizations within the University. Claiming that university students now shared the same ideology, the FEU president explained that there was no need for two parallel organizations and announced the fusion of the FEU and the UJC in a new body to be called the University Bureau, UJC–FEU. This process was to be repeated at the universities of Las Villas and Oriente.[44]

The joining together of all youth groups was only one phase of a larger fusion of Communists and Fidelistas and seems to indicate that as early as 1960 Castro was considering merging his 26th of July Movement with the PSP. In August, 1960, PSP Secretary General Blas Roca had advocated the union of all revolutionary forces in a single movement. It was not until

1962, however, that Fidelistas, Communists, and Directorio members formally merged into the Integrated Revolutionary Organizations (ORI), a preparatory step toward the creation of the United Party of the Socialist Revolution (PURS), later transformed into the Communist Party of Cuba (PCC)—the island's present ruling party.

This apparent harmony concealed an internal struggle for power. Although Castro had eliminated opposition outside the revolution, he still had to contend with inside factions that challenged his desire for absolute hegemony. Of these, the PSP was clearly the most dangerous. Throughout 1961 and part of 1962, Castro accepted the principle of "collective leadership," allowing old-guard Communists widespread control. By 1962, however, feeling his position threatened, Castro purged the old-time Communist leader Aníbal Escalante and moved toward direct personal control. In November, 1963, at a time when he leaned toward Communist China, Fidel appointed Juan Mier, Vice-Minister of Higher Education and a lesser PSP member, to replace the more important old-guard Communist leader Juan Marinello as Rector of the University of Havana.[45]

One episode in this power struggle brought into the open Communist maneuvers in the University of Havana student body. This was the trial of Marco ("Marquito") A. Rodríguez.* As a Communist informer Marquito had exposed the hideout of the four Directorio leaders assassinated by Batista's police on Humboldt Street on April 20, 1957. After fleeing to Mexico, he had received aid and protection from Joaquín Ordoqui and his wife, two leading PSP members. Ordoqui had obtained a scholarship for Marquito to study in Czechoslovakia and had helped him to become a member of the Juventud Socialista, the youth wing of the PSP. In 1961, at the insistence of the Directorio, which had discovered Marquito's guilt, Castro requested his arrest and extradition from Prague to Havana. Deported shortly thereafter, Marquito remained in jail in Cuba until his trial in March, 1964.

* See Chapter IV, note 73.

The trial—especially the testimony of Marquito—shed light on an important and previously unclear matter: the tactics of the PSP in dealing with the student movement during the 1955–1957 period. At first, the Communists had tried to infiltrate the Directorio. Marquito explained that the youth branch of the PSP had ordered him to concentrate on intelligence work within the Directorio. "All information," said the accused, "was transmitted to the University Bureau [the PSP group that worked within the University of Havana] to be sent on to its final destination . . . the Party." [46]

Later, in 1956, the Communists, realizing they could not gain control of the Directorio, had attempted to influence the creation of a "United Student Front" composed of delegates from the Directorio, the 26th of July Movement, and the PSP. The Communists had reasoned that any such front would reduce the Directorio's power and eventually fall under their own control. Marquito recounted the failure of that attempt and the differences that had arisen between the three factions. Finally, he explained the refusal of the Directorio to allow his participation in the plans for the Presidential Palace attack in 1957 and admitted having revealed the students' hideout to Batista's police. [47]

Castro used the trial to reassert his own power. He tried Marquito and took advantage of the opportunity to put the Communist PSP on the bench with the accused. All the top leaders of the PSP testified; they took pains to deny that the accused had been a member of the Juventud Socialista or had been connected with their party. Toward the end of the trial—perhaps thinking of his economic dependence on the Soviet Union and fearful of provoking Moscow's wrath—Fidel exonerated the PSP from guilt in the "Humboldt events" and ordered Marquito's execution. Whether Marquito had acted on his own initiative or followed the directives of the party when he betrayed the four students is still not known. The trial did, however, reveal that the Communists had used Marquito in their efforts to undermine the non-Communist revolutionary forces, especially the Directorio. [48]

Another challenge to Castro's authority arose early in 1966. This time it involved a full-fledged conspiracy within the armed forces led by the former president of the FEU, Major Rolando Cubela, and involving the exiled MRR leader Manuel Artime. The plotters planned to assassinate Castro, land an expedition under Artime's leadership, and establish a provisional regime with Cubela and Artime sharing top posts. Castro uncovered the conspiracy in March, 1966, arrested Cubela and six others, and sentenced them to long prison terms.[49]

The Cubela affair is significant for the disillusionment it revealed in a generation of students hitherto loyal to Castro. Cubela was well-known at the University of Havana and had been extremely popular there. During the trial, while the prosecution was requesting the death penalty for Cubela, students at the University demonstrated against the regime and distributed leaflets warning Castro that he would also die if Cubela were executed. The protests reached such a high pitch that Castro had to order the army to occupy the University. Many students were arrested; others were silenced by the threat of imprisonment. Perhaps aware that killing Cubela would only cause more resentment, Castro sent a letter to the prosecutor asking him not to insist on the death penalty. The tribunal obediently sentenced Cubela to twenty-five years in prison.[50]

In 1965, Castro's party (PURS) established its first cell at the University of Havana to ensure what Castro called the "second revolution" in Cuban education. The first one had involved the quantitative spread of educational facilities, and the second would focus on qualitative aspects, namely Marxist indoctrination.[51] Referring to the functions the party should perform at the University, party Organization Secretary Armando Hart explained that "the vanguard must promote the application of Communist methods of leadership within the whole university structure and advance the tasks demanded by the Revolution." These included, emphasized Hart, "work in ideological development, scientific preparation, and close ties to production and research." [52]

6
Universities and Students Under Castro

EDUCATIONAL AIMS: THE NEW SOCIALIST MAN

Faithful to Lenin's ideas that the school should "educate and prepare members of the Communist society," the Castro revolution is using education as the instrument to build the new society—to develop the socialist man. Speaking of the educational aims of the revolutionary regime, party Organization Secretary Armando Hart explained that the objective of socialist education was "the ideological, scientific and technical formation of whole generations capable of actively constructing socialism and communism." "The task of teaching and the ideological struggle are intimately related," he emphasized. "It is necessary to educate man against the individualistic ideology and to instill in him the work methods derived from the Marxist-Leninist concept." [1]

The creation of the new man required a change in the values and attitudes of most Cubans. Allegiance had to be transferred from the family to the party and to the fatherland. The faltering influence of the Church had to be eliminated completely. The aversion of the Cubans to manual labor, together with the tradition that women's place was in the home, had to be eradicated. The belief that events were determined by nature had to be transformed. And finally, the orientation toward the present had to be modified. At a ceremony installing a new University of Havana rector, Hart explained that every society was obliged to implant its own morals and that "the socialist society had the ethics of labor, science, and technology, which it is implanting with the backing and complete awareness of the masses." [2]

The new man and the new society envisioned by Castro and his regime would have to be significantly different. Devotion to the cause of communism and love of the fatherland would prevail. Man consciously would labor for the welfare of society. Each would work for all and all for each. The collective interest would supersede the individual one. "That is what is meant by revolution," explained Fidel, "that everyone shall benefit from the work of everyone else." [3] Racial prejudices would be eliminated. Honesty and truthfulness would guide everyone's life. The young would be taught to respect and admire party leaders, especially Fidel, and to obey party discipline. High consciousness of social duty and intolerance of violation of social interest would predominate. The new socialist morality would retain those characteristics developed by Castro's Rebel Army while fighting in the mountains against Batista. They included abnegation, a spirit of sacrifice, courage, and discipline. Speaking to a graduating class of teachers and after emphasizing that communism was not only a question of developing material wealth, but also of developing human awareness, Fidel described the type of man his regime proposed to create: "We will bring up human beings devoid of selfishness, devoid of defects of the past, human beings with a collective sense of effort, a collective sense of strength." [4]

The new society would be abundant in material wealth. But man would be less concerned with obtaining material goods for himself. He would rather work to produce for the whole society. "From an early age," explained Fidel, "children must be discouraged from every egotistical feeling in the enjoyment of material things such as the sense of individual property, and be encouraged toward the greatest common effort and the spirit of cooperation." [5] Not only is society to be abundant in material wealth, but money would be done away with. In a speech to the association of small farmers Castro explained his dream: ". . . there will arrive the day when money will have no value. Money is a vile intermediary between man and the products man creates." [6]

Not only money but other material incentives would be eliminated. Recalling Che Guevara's preaching emphasizing the superiority of moral over material incentives, an editorial in *Granma,* the official newspaper of Cuba's Communist Party, lashed at "economism," which it described as "the tendency to consider that men produced more and better as they received more and better." The new Communist ideology, explained the editorial, will not be imposed through talks, guidance, or meetings only but through a gigantic effort to organize the productive, social, educational, and cultural activity of the Cuban people. "Men produce more and better," concluded *Granma,* "as they improve the organization of work, as technical training is improved, technological and scientific resources are more extensively employed, and Communist awareness becomes greater." [7]

In foreign affairs the Cuban masses would have to be irreconciliably opposed to the enemies of the fatherland, especially to the United States. The Cubans would show solidarity with the peoples of developing countries, of the socialist camp, and particularly, of Latin America as well as friendship and brotherhood toward the peoples of the Soviet Union. An American reporter visiting Cuba in mid-1967 was shocked at the campaign of hate against the United States. "The saddest thing about the Cuban revolution," wrote James Reston, "is that it is teaching hate and violence to the young. A remarkable new generation of Cubans, more literate and disciplined than any other, is being indoctrinated systematically with the idea that the United States is the embodiment of everything that is narrow, selfish, and evil in the world today." [8] Richard R. Fagen has pointed out, furthermore, that the new Cuba would be largely defined as "the antithesis of the old Cuba, bastard child of the United States." [9]

All efforts had to be directed toward committing the younger generation to these principles. If the drive to create the new man failed, then the revolution would fail too. For the creation of the ideal society depended on the success of the educational system. The millenium could not be reached without creating the proper attitudes. And the Castro regime seemed convinced that under the direction of the party education could be used as an indispensable tool in developing the new socialist man.

It is too early to tell how successful the regime has been in rooting out the old habits and the old values. Less than a decade of revolution can hardly be expected to have destroyed all that was "bad" in Cuba's cultural legacy. In his July 26, 1967, speech, Castro confessed that the greatest obstacle had been creating the "proper way of thinking" in the present generation. "There remains," said Fidel, comparing his present struggle against the "vices of the past" to his 1953 attack on the Santiago military barracks, "the most difficult Moncada of all, the Moncada of the old ideas, of old selfish sentiments, of old habits of thinking and ways of viewing everything, and this fortress has not been completely taken." [10]

This attack on the past has not meant a total rejection of Cuba's cultural tradition. On the contrary, the Castro regime emphasizes certain aspects of the past, such as Negro and native cultural contributions as well as Cuban sacrifices at the time of the wars of independence. The cult of Martí has continued unabated, though Martí's writings have been carefully screened to select those which showed his anti-Americanism and his admiration for some socialistic ideas. The revolution's efforts at cultural changes are taking a nationalistic direction. It seems as if the Castro regime is attempting to find, in what it considers "good" in Cuba's past, a new identity. This search for a nationalistic identity is definitely influencing Cuba's present cultural direction and certainly will shape the thinking of the new socialist man.

It is not too early to note that the new intelligentsia emerging now in Cuba will be significantly different from that of pre-Castro times. The latter was cosmopolitan and had been exposed to both Western and Eastern ideas. It came usually from middle- or upper-class families. A part, although still small, of the new Cuban intelligentsia is coming mostly from worker backgrounds and, in some instances, from rural environments. Its view of other cultures, particularly that of the United States, has been deliberately distorted to fit the objectives of the Cuban Communist Party. Understanding of other cultures and their problems has been hampered, furthermore, by the nature of the available reading materials and by the educational efforts of the Castro regime.

THE SOCIAL AND
EDUCATIONAL APPARATUS

Educating the young involved more than what the school could offer. The whole of society had to be geared toward producing the proper conditions for the development of the new man. A massive social apparatus was thus developed to mold the mind of the growing generation. It included the press, the mass communication media, social, cultural, and workers organizations, and even the Unidades Militares de Ayuda a la Producción (UMAP or forced labor camps). The party, the UJC, the army all provide political instruction. At all levels of life Cubans are exposed to political instruction. Writing in the theoretical journal *Cuba Socialista,* Edith García Buchaca indicated the regime's awareness of the important role movies, radio, television, and the press played in the "cultural and ideological formation of the masses." [11] University of Oriente Rector José Antonio Portuondo, writing also in *Cuba Socialista,* reiterated that the efforts of all the revolutionary leaders, beginning with Fidel Castro, were directed at making radio and television "informational and educational vehicles through which the masses could be both *informed* and *formed*." [12]

Aware also that one of the most stubborn obstacles to the ideological conversion of the Cuban people was the cultural and political legacy of the past, fully documented in the works of Cuban writers, the Castro government launched a purge of all literature incompatible with the Communist view. Not only were old textbooks eliminated but many were rewritten to justify the Castro revolution and its movement into the Communist camp. The government also embarked on a massive effort to divulge the writings of foreign and particularly Communist and Socialist writers.[13]

Before his death in Bolivia in 1967, Che Guevara described how the educational system worked in Cuba. The process of educating the young, Guevara explained, was twofold: on the one hand society acted upon the individual by means of direct and indirect education while, on the other hand, the individual underwent a conscious phase of self-education. Guevara differentiated between what he called direct and indirect education. Direct education was the job performed by educational institutions, the party information organs, the mass media. Indirect education consisted mainly in the pressure exerted by the educated masses and the social apparatus on the uneducated individual. "The individual receiving the impact of the social power," wrote Guevara, "realizes his inadequacy and tries to adjust to a situation. He is educating himself." [14]

Schools at all levels formed the core of the social apparatus. But before schools could be effective the old "bourgeois" intelligentsia had to be either eliminated or won over, the schools had to be transformed, and a whole generation of teachers had to be prepared.

To eliminate the old intelligentsia was relatively easy. Some members of this group left the country voluntarily during the first years of the revolution. Others were expelled, purged, or pensioned from their bureaucratic and academic positions.

Still others, who accepted the regime, were at first incorporated only to be later replaced by more trustworthy younger cadres. Why Castro allowed the old intelligentsia to leave Cuba requires some explanation. Underlying the regime's thinking was the assumption that a generation reared under the capitalist system could not be trusted or converted to Marxism-Leninism. Every disloyal intellectual that left therefore could be substituted by a loyal follower. In addition, a policy of allowing Cubans to leave the island acted as an escape valve, diminishing opposition and releasing internal pressures. Undoubtedly a disloyal group of writers, professors, intellectuals, and *pensadores* could influence public opinion and become a source of potential trouble.

The decimation of the old intelligentsia was accompanied by a decrease in university enrollment. Affected by revolutionary measures or dissatisfied with the regime, many students dropped out of the universities or left the country. Scores of students, furthermore, accepted governmental jobs or volunteered to teach in the new schools that were being established.[15]

The government was faced with a serious manpower shortage. If the goals of economic development were to be realized, there was need to develop the necessary technical personnel. Instead of the old liberal arts university, a new technologically oriented institution had to be created. "A university," Hart explained, "that would be completely integrated into the production and the life of the country . . . that would leave the old buildings and proceed directly to working in production, to helping production, and to research in production." [16]

Autonomy was the greatest obstacle to transforming the universities. An autonomous institution ruled by its old faculty and allowed to develop its own educational program was totally incompatible with the regime's objectives. Despite numerous assertions that it intended to respect this closely guarded tradition of most Latin American universities, the Castro regime intervened in Cuba's higher educational institutions, converting them into appendages of the state. Former University of Havana Rector, Salvador Vilaseca, issued the most categorical denial of the principle of autonomy made by any Castro official. "In countries like Cuba," explained Vilaseca, "where the people are running the country through their government machine, university autonomy is really something that is quite inconsistent. The university is a part of the state . . . it is under the Ministry of Education, which determines its general policy and which correctly fits the university into overall educational plans." [17]

The bitter struggle between State and gown that took place during the first two years of the revolution has been abundantly explained. The take over of the universities and the abolition of their autonomy was, however, only one step in a major reform plan. On January 10, 1962, the anniversary of Mella's death, the government proclaimed a comprehensive university reform plan. It had taken the Higher Council of Universities, organized in December, 1960, almost two years to prepare the reform plan. With minor modifications, discussed below, this reform plan served as the foundation for the organization of higher education in Cuba.[18]

THE UNIVERSITY REFORM

The changes implemented were far-reaching. All university instruction was concentrated in the universities of Havana, Las Villas, and Oriente. Former private colleges and universities were abolished or nationalized. Science and applied technology were greatly emphasized. Instruction took on a more practical and experimental character. Emphasis shifted to practical rather than theoretical studies. Polytechnical training and socially useful work was stressed. Instructors were expected to relate classroom work to practice. Numerous students were accomodated in special houses and supplied with scholarships. In accordance with Marxist pedagogical interpretation, provisions were made for the student to gain experience and engage in productive work during his educational years. Finally, the programs of study were designed to prepare specialists of high quality rather than to give a broad education in the sciences and the humanities. Vilaseca stressed that "the main function of the university was to train man with a Communist awareness in the domination of science and technology." [19]

The universities directed their efforts to help develop specific areas of the national economy, such as agro-livestock genetics, chemistry, sucrochemistry, and energetics. In addition, they promoted research and experimentation in every possible branch of science and the linking of education to every area of industry and agriculture. "The traditional scientific isolation of our university teachings," explained Hart, "is an evil we must combat, but we must not fall into the opposite error of exclusively leaning toward pure practice and forgetting the indispensable theoretical formation." [20]

The task of directing the universities fell to the National Council of Universities, which was composed of faculty and student representatives from the three universities and of representatives from the government. Presided over by the Minister of Education, the Council has been guiding all administrative and academic decisions as well as planning changes in higher educational programs.

The Council worked very closely with university rectors, who continued to be, as in the past, the highest authority within the university. Appointed now by the government, rectors of the three universities implemented the Council's directives and handled the universitys' academic and administrative affairs. They were aided by three vice-rectors in charge of instructional affairs, scientific studies, and research and administration, respectively. A communiqué issued by the Council placed on the rector more responsibility for directing the universities, adding "that Rectors and Vice-Rectors must jointly analyze the problems, with the aim of applying, correctly, the policy directed at each university." [21]

The internal organization of the universities was altered considerably. The reform movement abolished the old *cátedra por asignatura* (professorial chair) that aspiring faculty members used to obtain through *oposiciones* (professorial competitions). In its place, departments were organized to group professors of a similar discipline. Several departments formed a school, and the joining of schools resulted in the *facultad*.[22]

Oddly enough, this new organization resembles to a large degree American universities. Cuban officials, however, refuse to admit the similarity. "The Cuban university," explained university professor and member of the secretariat of the Cuban Communist Party Carlos Rafael Rodríguez, "will not have as a model the North American universities where academic work is disconnected, scattered in departments. On the contrary, the Cuban university will be perfectly integrated." [23]

Whereas the facultad became primarily an administrative unit, the school assumed an important educational task. In each school teacher's committees were organized to orient, inspect, and evaluate the work of students and professors and to supervise the work of the school in general. A Junta de Gobierno (Governing Council), presided over by the dean of the facultad with the participation of three professors and two representatives from the student body, ruled the facultades.

By allowing the existence of this *co-gobierno* (co-government of student and professors), the regime had institutionalized, at least temporarily, this peculiar feature of many Latin American universities. There are several reasons for Castro's acceptance of co-gobierno. The demand for co-gobierno went back to the university reform movement of 1923 when students requested a voice in running the university. The anti-Batista student generation, which during the first years of the revolution participated actively in shaping university policies, also shared this objective. It was difficult now for the government to deny this highly politicized generation a role in university government.

There were, furthermore, other important reasons for allowing co-gobierno. Although the campuses had been "purified" of counterrevolutionary professors, there still remained some who resisted the rapid socialization and the innovations taking place at the universities. Loyal students had to be placed in key positions to insure the faculty's "proper attitude." Students' role in decision-making also became a force for academic reform since students shared enthusiastically the government's desire to modernize and upgrade the universities. Finally, by providing an outlet for student grievances, cogobierno encouraged action within rather than against the university. Vilaseca pointed out that co-gobierno enabled the teaching authorities to get acquainted with student problems. "The presence of students in the university administration," explained Vilaseca, "constitutes a constant source of mobilization for the students because of the new battles that must be fought against outdated teaching methods." [24]

Vilaseca's view of co-gobierno, however, is not shared by all Castro officials. Carlos Rafael Rodríguez, one of the guiding forces behind the reform plans, always considered co-gobierno a temporary feature of university administration. Writing in 1962, Rodríguez explained that a professor of revolutionary conscience and oriented by Marxism-Leninism will not need the students' watchful presence "since he will have sufficient maturity to focus educational problems with the right judgment." [25] Whether the government's commitment to co-gobierno was motivated by the above mentioned considerations or by a real desire to institutionalize the procedure is difficult to tell. The evident tendency of the past years has been, however, toward a decrease in the students' role in decision-making.

A most interesting change is that of the old Escuela de Ciencias Sociales y Derecho Público. What formerly was called Social Sciences now is called Political Science. Following the pattern set by other Communist countries, this change not only signals a specialization in the direction of political science but also the "politization" of the social sciences and the introduction of political premises and purpose into the social sciences.[26]

The primary aim of the school is not the formation of political cadres, a task left to the party and to the Escuelas de Instrucción Revolucionaria (EIR), but the training of those who already fulfill political or governmental functions. Students for the school are not chosen by means of open competition but are carefully selected by party and government organizations in accordance with their immediate needs. Before entering the school, students must be "selfless, devoted to study, of proven political qualification, and selected by certain ministries of the revolutionary government." [27]

Another interesting development has been the establishment of the Institute of Economics at the University of Havana. The Institute is a combination of the old Facultad de Ciencias Comerciales and of the Instituto Superior de Estudios Económicos which had been created in the mid-1950's. It offers two basic courses of study leading to the degrees of either Economist or Public Accountant. A special course in planning, lasting three semesters, was set up to prepare technicians "with a minimum of knowledge for simpler tasks in government enterprises." [28] Since most of the graduates from this Institute play an important role in economic planning or are used as counselors, advisers, and administrators in various enterprises, the government is particularly interested in developing in them both an understanding of the functioning of the new society and a specially strong loyalty to the principles of Marxism-Leninism.

IDEOLOGICAL ORIENTATION:
THE EMPHASIS ON MARXISM-LENINISM

Together with this reorganization there occurred important innovations in the content of university education. The government introduced two indoctrination-oriented courses: Materialismo Dialéctico e Histórico (Dialectical and Historical Materialism) and Economía Política (Political Economy). Students in every field of study are required to take the Materialism course for the first three semesters and Political Economy for the succeeding two. The government is fully aware that these courses are not enough to convert university students to Marxism. The courses are aimed primarily at acquainting the student with Marxist-Leninist thinking and at placing him in the "proper road toward Marxism." "Our youth will become Marxist," explained Carlos Rafael Rodríguez, "through life itself, under the influence of socioeconomic transformations taking place as well as under the influence of classes and books." [29]

The regime, however, does not wait passively for the students' discovery and acceptance of Marxism. In addition to the two specialized courses, the whole curriculum emphasizes the regime's political orientation. Liberal arts courses are taught through the Marxist prism and teachers are expected to show an awareness of and a dedication to Marxist-Leninist dogma. It is in the humanities and the social sciences in general and in history in particular where the greatest effort is being undertaken to develop Communist awareness. History is used to foster patriotism and to develop an acceptance "of the scientific law of the inevitability of the downfall of capitalism and the victory of communism." Writing in *Cuba Socialista*, Hart explained that materialism as a philosophical concept of the world must be the basic and indisputable premise of every program of study. After describing the importance of Marxism-Leninism for university studies he added:

> It is not enough that every program should respond in its general outline to the principles of dialectical and historical materialism. Every student must additionally acquire a knowledge of Marxism-Leninism by studying this discipline in order to organize the knowledge acquired in other subjects and thus verify the methods and veracity of its laws, while at the same time being able to clarify the knowledge acquired in each particular branch of science. [30]

Implementing Marxist-Leninist teachings has not been without difficulties. Criticism emerged in 1966 from a small though vocal group within the University of Havana's Department of Philosophy. Fidel had recruited several young Cuban intellectuals in 1963 for the task of organizing a Department of Philosophy "free of any dogmatic influence." Following the Havana Tricontinental Conference of January 1966 and at a time when he was feuding with the Soviet Union, Fidel attempted to strike out on an independent ideological line and decided to use the University of Havana as a shield for his campaign.

The work of the group clashed with the methods of instruction employed by the Escuelas de Instrucción Revolucionaria (EIR), the schools to train party cadres directed by old-guard PSP leader Lionel Soto. A very revealing polemic developed. In the monthly magazine *El caimán barbudo,* the Department attacked the manuals on Marxist philosophy by Soviet authors Costantinov and Nikitin that were being used by the EIR and had been widely distributed in Cuba to resolve urgent problems connected with the dissemination and application of Marx's and Lenin's ideas.[31]

The EIR responded to the challenge of the members of the Department of Philosophy by publishing in *Teoría y Práctica,* the EIR's theoretical journal, an article entitled "¿Contra el manualismo? ¿Contra los manuales? ¿O contra la enseñanza del Marxismo-Leninismo?" (Against Manualism? Against Manuals? Or Against the Teaching of Marxism-Leninism?). In an introduction to the article, Soto explained that they were trying to face up to the definite solution of the question of using the manuals in a "Marxist, realist, and proletarian manner." The article defended the use of the manual emphasizing that the entire substance of Fidel Castro's thinking and of the line of the Cuban revolution could be understood through the manuals. The article concluded by recommending "a critical use of the manuals," adding that it was up to the professors to use them with intelligence and to apply the lessons in these manuals to the reality of Cuba.

Aurelio Alonso, of the Department of Philosophy, soon replied to the EIR. Writing also in *Teoría y Práctica,* he pointed out that the attack had not been at the manual as such, but "against what the manual had become between certain historical periods." "The manual to be fought against," explained Alonso, "is the manual that would present an abridged version of the construction of a philosophical system that claims to be the organic synthesis of the thinking of Marx, Engels, and Lenin, and that instead turns out to be a restricted policy of cultural regimentation." After explaining that the manual breaks with the historical criterion in order to return to the absolute criterion which Marx himself had rejected, Alonso summarized the essence of the polemic:

> We must once again make a choice between a type of Marxism which claims to solve the problems of the future with the solutions of the past and a Marxism which invites us to study the solutions of the past in a critical fashion and which would thus tend first of all to reject those manuals which are the products of that practical and sometimes distorted application of the thinking of Karl Marx and V. I. Lenin.

The struggle brought into the open two very different types of intellectuals emerging in Castro's Cuba. The one is docile, willing to accept uncritically the Marxist dogma. The other is rebellious, unwilling to think through preordained channels and unwilling to reject completely its own culture to accept a cannonized Marxist one. The challenge is not only academic but primarily political, for it is this new generation which will guide the future course of revolution.

At 28 years of age, Aurelio Alonso is only partially representative of the new Cuban intelligentsia. His skepticism and critical attitude is in part a manifestation of the ideological weakness of the Cuban revolution, but it is primarily a reflection of Castro's desire to reassert his individuality within the Communist world.

In a speech at the inauguration of the San Andrés experimental elementary school on January 28, 1967, Fidel reaffirmed his independent ideological line. He explained that in the face of reactionary ideas, even oftentimes disguised by Marxist-Leninist terminology, the Cubans held their own revolutionary ideas. "We will be in the vanguard of revolutionary ideas," said Fidel, "in the vanguard on the path toward socialism, toward communism. That does not mean we have proposed to leave the rest behind. But if the rest lags behind, we are not responsible. If we change simply because we want to do things better, and find ourselves in the revolutionary and ideological vanguard, we are not to blame." [32]

The effect of the political courses at the universities are reenforced by the activities of the Union of Young Communists (UJC). The University Bureaus, UJC-FEU organize circles or meetings for further study and discussion of Marxism-Leninism. There are also special evening lectures on particular subjects such as the international situation. The Union's newspaper, *Juventud Rebelde,* is an important vehicle for disseminating ideological indoctrination and party directives. On bulletin boards and walls throughout the campus, newspaper clippings and party slogans are displayed. The UJC, furthermore, reenforces other agencies engaged in moral education, in improving scholarship, and in maintaining discipline.

The UJC is also an important agent of social mobilization and social control. It assists university authorities and others in conducting physical education, sports, and military training programs. It has played a key role in persuading youths to "volunteer" for sugarcane cutting or for the 1968 revolutionary offensive. (The revolutionary offensive was an all-out attempt by the Castro regime to increase production as well as to enforce greater ideological purity). Perhaps one of its most important functions is recruiting and molding youths for important positions later on in party and government organizations.[33]

An important feature not only of university education but

also of the whole educational system is the emphasis on competition. This takes the form not of competition of individual against individual but of group against group, or of a group against past performance. Competition, which the Cubans call emulation, is stimulated by a variety of incentives, ranging from an honorary mention in the school's bulletin to a paid vacation. In organized sports and recreation and in educational endeavors youngsters are trained from early age to respond to these rewards.

As in the past, a college degree continues to enjoy great prestige in Cuba. Cuban society still regards a university education very highly, and the regime considers it as the principal method of channeling the abilities of the nation. Attendance at a university is a prized opportunity, and many individuals seem to consider this opportunity as indispensable to significant advancement. Not only students but the faculties enjoy great dignity in Cuba's new Communist society. A professorial job carries, in addition to considerable amount of prestige, many of the rewards reserved for the governmental elite.

Also, the University of Havana continues in its traditional predominant position as the center of higher learning in Cuba. The government has attempted to increase the educational role played by the other two universities. New programs of study have been initiated and new faculties have been added at the universities of Las Villas and Oriente. Despite this progress, they lag behind in both prestige and academic standards. The University of Havana still enjoys a better faculty augmented by a number of foreign professors, fine physical facilities, and an ideal location in the capital city. These factors are undoubtedly helping to maintain its predominant position and to attract students.

TEACHER SHORTAGE

One of the greatest obstacles encountered by the revolution

in developing its educational plans was the lack of qualified teachers, especially in the fields of science and technology. The flight of numerous teachers during the early years of the revolution, together with the struggle for control of the universities which resulted in the resignation of large part of their faculties, added to an already precarious situation. The widespread teaching of Marxism also created a demand for teachers versed in this field. In dire need of professors, the government found itself forced to curtail university programs, recruit less qualified professionals, and import educators from Latin America, eastern Europe, or other parts of the world to teach at the universities. Writing in *Cuba Socialista,* Hart complained that the greatest obstacle the government faced in developing technical education was the lack of such a tradition. After recognizing that a tradition of technological education at the university had existed but only to train "small groups of students as engineers and architects," Hart explained that except for a small group of teachers there were few with any experience in the formation of technicians at the intermediate level.[34]

Unlike the specialized programs to train teachers for primary and secondary education, there are no programs to prepare university professors. Teachers who have proven their capacity teaching in secondary schools or professionals who have gained prestige in their profession are hired to teach at the universities. Students in their last years of study are trained by their professors and used as instructors in most departments.

Encouraged by the Cuban government, many foreign educators and specialists, particularly from eastern and western Europe and Latin America, are teaching at Cuban universities. There are also several émigrés from the Spanish Civil War offering courses. These faculty members have been involved in setting up programs, study materials, and texts and training professors, as well as giving classes to the student body. A former student and instructor in the University of Havana's Facultad of Technology claims that most Latin American faculty members are not really Marxists or Communists, but opportunists who are underemployed in their countries. "They receive," he added, "a good salary and good treatment, so they spend a nice time in Cuba." [35]

As part of exchange agreements between Cuban and Soviet universities, Cuban professors have been giving courses to Russian students in the Soviet Union, and several Soviet professors teach at Cuban universities. Two professors from the University of Havana School of History have been offering courses in modern and contemporary Latin American History at Lomonosov University in Moscow. Also at Lomonosov, María Cristina Miranda, a Spanish-Soviet educator who spent four years in Cuba, has been training Russian students in Latin American and Cuban history. Following an agreement with the Cuban Ministry of Education several of her students are now teaching at the University of Havana. [36]

Russian universities are not the only ones providing aid to Cuban institutions. East European universities have signed continuous agreements on technical collaboration and mutual assistance with Cuban institutions. These agreements include exchange of books, technical information, professors, and material. [37]

Faculty tenure has been eliminated at all Cuban universities. Faculty members are hired on the basis of an annual contract which can be terminated at any time. Since the government is in great need of qualified teachers, retirements are postponed as long as possible. During vacation time the less qualified faculty members are required to take courses to upgrade their intellectual level. In addition to increasing knowledge and improving teaching techniques, the courses also include their dose of Marxist indoctrination. [38] High school and primary school teachers are also encouraged to take these specialized courses at the universities. They are paid their full salary while taking the courses, and those completing them receive a salary increase. "These economic incentives plus the coercive power of the regime," explained Delfín González, an elementary school teacher, "are definitely much more effective than all the moral incentives being offered." [39]

SCHOLARSHIPS BY LOYALTY

The size of the student body at the universities is not determined by chance or pressure from the students, but by the number of specialists required. Although during the first few years of the revolution admission to a university was not restricted, the Castro regime did not follow an "open-door" admission policy similar to that followed by the Bolsheviks after coming to power in Russia.[40] Profiting perhaps from the Russian experience, which resulted in lower academic standards and increased student opposition, the Cuban regime decided to train a more selective group. Although tuition was eliminated, since 1962 requirements for admission have grown stiffer. They include, in addition to the customary transcripts from earlier schools, an entrance examination, a test to determine "revolutionary attitude," a personal interview, and, in some instances, a report from the CDR (Committee for the Defense of the Revolution) or other mass organization.

Few obstacles are put in the way of young people who want to pursue degrees in engineering or medicine. But there is much emphasis on the part of vocational guidance counselors that is creating in children and youth an interest in courses of study related to the agricultural-livestock industry, the fishing industry, and the teaching profession. For the development of these and other disciplines, the government is willing to make a substantial investment.

The scholarship program is providing students who in the past had been unable to attend the university with an opportunity to obtain a higher education.[41] Although before the revolution university tuition charges were extremely modest, the cost of books and other study materials and of lodgings made it arduous for students of lower income families or from rural areas to attend the universities. In addition, many of these students had to find full-time employment, thus reducing their available time to study. The establishment in the 1950's of the universities of Las Villas and Oriente alleviated this situation somewhat. Students, however, continued to be attracted toward the University of Havana, which offered a greater variety of courses, had better facilities, enjoyed a higher prestige, and was located in the capital.

To apply for a government grant a candidate must be in need of financial aid. He must agree to hold the scholarship for a minimum of two years, comply with the teaching discipline, and maintain a high academic average. In order to retain the grant, he must pass every course and devote a number of hours a week to individual study. A scholarship holder's obligations include "study, attend classes every day, raise his political and cultural level, comply with the teaching discipline, and be ready to defend the revolution at any time." [42] One other obligation not specified by the government in scholarship announcements is voluntary work. Scholarship holders are required to devote time to "socially-productive tasks." The universities organized so-called Red Brigades of Voluntary Work to group students for work in industry and agriculture. Evenings, weekends, and holidays students spend time in productive tasks.

There are two types of scholarships. One type includes lodging in special housing facilities—usually large apartment buildings or large houses belonging to former members of the "old bourgeoisie"—clothing, food, books, medical care, and a monthly allowance for personal expenses. These scholarship holders are only allowed to leave their dormitories to attend classes, on Sundays, or by special permit. The other type of scholarship is available primarily to supplement the income of working students. In addition to books, these students receive a monthly allowance. [43]

There are also scholarships for study abroad. These, however, are limited to the more promising and trustworthy students. Since the regime is afraid that students might defect, requirements for scholarships in non-Communist countries are far more rigid than for Communist nations. [44]

The lives of scholarship holders are very active. Their time is apportioned for studies, care of the dormitories, "voluntary work," and recreation. Dances and cultural events are held as well as study circles to achieve political orientation. An obviously enthusiastic Peruvian scholarship holder studying at the University of Havana described the life of his colleagues. "In order to understand the true significance of the Plan of University Scholarships," this student said, "it would really be necessary to live with us, to sense the great brotherhood that is created through living and studying together, to share in the moments of happiness and difficulties, and to join with us in similar longings and objectives . . ." [45]

This rather romantic view of a foreign student contrasts sharply with the disciplined and demanding life of Cuban scholarship holders. In a meeting of the Union of Young Communists (UJC) its leaders suggested to university administration the application of rules of discipline for all university students. The UJC agreed to study students' attitudes before every course "so as to have sufficient grounds for judgment at the moment any action is taken against them." The UJC further suggested that students be assigned a minimum of twenty hours weekly to study and that they [UJC] would be watchful that this task be carried out completely.[46]

Obviously, the government's scholarship program is totally reserved for applicants loyal to the revolution. Students must evidence unqualified devotion to the party not only before applying for a scholarship, but also throughout its duration. For those students willing to conform, the future is full of opportunity. All others, and they seem to be a minority, are alienated, mistrusted. They live under the shadow of disgrace, fearful of being arrested or expelled. In the field of higher education, the Castro regime is determined to prevent any opposition while giving every opportunity to loyal students. As Castro bluntly put it: "To train a university-educated technician costs thousands upon thousands of pesos . . . should we train technicians who are later going to leave to work in the United States? I don't believe that's right." [47]

The scholarship program, particularly the system of boarding schools and the requirement that students engage in productive work, are of extreme political importance. Through them the party is attempting to accomplish several objectives. First, to destroy the old aversion of students to manual labor and to generate enthusiasm for the revolutionary economic goals. Second, to expand ideological indoctrination. Third, to increase production, thus alleviating food shortages. Fourth, to promote a collective feeling and a sense of discipline, as well as to destroy the students' attachment to the city. Finally, to break up the family, therefore tightening the influence of the state.

STUDENTS AND THE MILITARY

An interesting innovation in higher education is the amount of military training required of the students. Although students are exempted from military service as such, they must undergo a measure of military training during the period of their studies. They are required to devote several hours each week to military drill and the use of small arms. Physical training is an important part of these exercises, and the government emphasizes gymnastics as an important factor in the training of the young. Students are also expected to participate in some "para-military organization" such as the militia. Special provisions are made, furthermore, for the students to undertake joint ventures with the FAR (Revolutionary Armed Forces). University of Oriente students, for example, have been participating, together with members of the political section of the army, in agricultural tasks.[48]

The government has increasingly been recruiting students for the FAR. The growing complexity of the military establishment and the sophisticated weaponry being shipped to Cuba by the Soviet Union has changed the nature of the Cuban armed forces requiring personnel of technical ability. Although several military academies exist, the government has been turning to the universities and to the secondary schools for this needed personnel.[49] Announcements in the mass media continuously exhort the students to follow a military career. One such article in *Granma* appealed to the students' patriotism. "You will have," the article said, "the high honor of fighting for and defending your fatherland, bearing arms, and having a command of the most modern techniques." [50]

The FAR is in particular need of doctors and medical assistants. In 1966 it organized a School of Military Medicine under the auspices of the University of Havana's Facultad of Medical Sciences. Through the UJC, the FAR recruited qualified students to undergo the military medical apprenticeship. These students were provided scholarships specially created by Minister of the Armed Forces Raúl Castro.[51]

Underlying this emphasis on military training is the regime's desire to prevent a return to the militarism of the past and to develop among the young the values and attitudes of Cuba's new military elite. The fear that the military might become, as in the past, a contender for power is very present in Castro's mind. One way in which his regime is preventing this from happening is by involving the military into every aspect of the country's life. The military engages in a variety of extracurricular activities and in a number of joint projects with various groups, particularly with the students. Through these contacts the government hopes that military values such as discipline, loyalty, and a spirit of sacrifice will be passed on to the young. "We believe that one of the immediate benefits of the close relationship between the military Communist youth and the civilian," explained UJC Secretary Crombet, "will be to strengthen and increase the fighting spirit of each one of our young people." [52]

THE WORKER-FARMER FACULTAD

An interesting phenomenon in Cuba's higher educational

development under Castro was the establishment of the Facultad Obrera y Campesina at the University of Havana in 1963. Inspired by Mella's "Popular University José Martí" and by the Soviet rabfac,[53] the Facultad Obrera prepares workers and peasants for enrollment in specific university divisions and for positions in industrial and agricultural enterprises. Faced with a shortage of trained personnel, aware that workers and peasants were not qualified to attend the university in many instances even after completing secondary education, and unwilling to trust the "children of the bourgeoisie," the government created this preparatory program.

The Facultad Obrera was regarded as a powerful weapon to produce loyal technocrats and to be used against the "old intelligentsia." Courses are oriented to train workers in technical and scientific studies on a level higher than or equal to that of secondary education. In general, the programs of study are tailored to fit the government needs in specific areas of production. The physical sciences form the nucleus of the curriculum. The curriculum is distributed in such a way that in the three years the program lasts students acquire the indispensable knowledge for taking more advanced courses. The curriculum also includes social science courses and an introduction to Marxism-Leninism course.

Admission is limited to organized workers or peasants and to personnel of the ministries of Industries and of the Armed Forces. Students must be at least eighteen years old and pass a competitive entrance examination. Organized workers are required to include with their application for admission an official statement from the Cuban Workers' Confederation certifying "a conscientious and revolutionary attitude toward work and defense and an interest in cultural and technical improvement." [54]

The courses emphasize practical teaching. Classes are taught not only in the school buildings but also in factories, by means of periodic visits. This activity outside the classroom has been complicated by lack of transportation facilities and by the limited time available during evening classes. The government has attempted to remedy the situation by holding classes at the factories.[55] Absenteeism and lack of organization, however, has plagued the Facultad Obrera.

A more complicated problem is the lack of a qualified faculty. Without a systematic teacher-training program, teachers have to be drawn from other educational institutions or improvised according to need.[56] Professors are grouped into departments. Each department organizes its "teacher's collective" for the purpose of discussing teaching problems. These collectives plan, organize, and coordinate the course work, working out didactic guidelines. They evaluate the work accomplished by the collective itself, the individual work of each professor, the study materials utilized, and the scholastic progress of the students. Faculty, administrators, and student representatives meet periodically in a plenary assembly to examine critically teaching, ideological, and administrative matters.

In the beginning this type of institution was limited to Havana. But, aware of the need for this kind of instruction in other parts of the country, the government established Facultades Obreras in the other two universities and created numerous other units.[57]

STUDENT ATTITUDES AND BEHAVIOR

With the Communist Party of Cuba directing student activities and the universities shorn of their autonomy and geared to socioeconomic development, student involvement in politics has reached a low ebb. Castro unquestionably enjoys student support, but its intensity and extent cannot be accurately determined. Student opposition has been contained primarily by the coercive strength of the Castro regime. Dissident students are periodically purged, strict discipline is imposed by student militias and other repressive forces, and "counterrevolutionaries" are strictly prevented from enrolling in the universities.[58]

Other factors can also be adduced to explain the present lack of student political opposition. First, the regime maintains the students, and for that matter the entire Cuban population, in a state of emergency and mobilization. Castro's propaganda incessantly warns that Cuba is surrounded by powerful enemies, that the future of the revolution is at stake. Students share in the continuous mass mobilizations and spend many weekends cutting sugarcane in the fields. These and other extracurricular activities required by the government exhaust the students' energy and leave little time for politics.

These activities have also been a factor in reducing time available for study. A questionnaire administered to eighty-eight University of Oriente geology students showed that lack of time ranked highest (30.9%) among the most bothersome problems faced by the students.[59] Recently UJC-FEU leaders have been emphasizing academic excellence as one of the students' most important goals. "There is a victory we must win," said University of Havana UJC Secretary General, "and this is to form in the student the habit of daily and thorough study of his subjects." [60]

Castro's constant exhortations to the students to participate in extracurricular chores and his criticism of "pampered youths who lack a revolutionary conscience and willingness to work for society" may indicate a decrease in nation-building enthusiasm. Not only Fidel but also the party has to emphasize constantly the need to struggle against "cheating, laziness, absenteeism, and lack of discipline." [61] Apparently, university students still retain their elitist, middle-class attitude toward manual labor. More than the abstract goal of "working for society," what probably motivates them is ambition and a mixture of fear and hope for the future. Furthermore, the charismatic appeal exerted by Castro has probably eroded over time; today many students may have grown apathetic and immune to the regime's constant revolutionary exhortations.

There is evidence to indicate an aversion on the part of many students and youngsters in general to becoming politically involved. They want to be free from the demands and exhortations of the party. Even among UJC activists there seems to be a decreasing interest in Marxist theory and an increasing boredom with the leaders of the revolution. Within the organization, there exists a hard core group of dedicated activists. These young people are totally devoted to the cause of the revolution. Possessed with a missionary zeal, they work incessantly for its advancement, leading austere lives and willing to offer time and effort to the party's call. They seem motivated by a combination which includes ambition, a feeling of participation, and admiration for Fidel. Their numbers, however, are small, and UJC leaders are constantly attempting to project this zeal to the rest of the members. UJC Secretary General, Jaime Crombet, complained in a speech to UJC activists that the cadres of his organization were not studying, reading, or analyzing, and explained that he had been shocked to learn that nearly all the members of the UJC Provincial Bureau had not read Raúl Castro's latest speech, "one of his most profound speeches." "There exists a tendency toward pragmatism . . ." said Crombet, "but this should not be accompanied by neglect of a thorough knowledge of Marxism-Leninism." [62]

The UJC seems to have produced also an inhibiting feeling even among its own militants. Its activists are afraid to express themselves or to assume any independent action. Since "wrong" actions or opinions might result in harsh criticism or expulsion from the organization, they have adopted a do-little-say-nothing attitude. Crombet complained about those comrades "who feel a bit fearful and when sometimes they fail or make a mistake in their work they feel that someone is coming to 'shoot them.' " Crombet exhorted UJC members to substitute a spirit of confidence and comradeship for this fear and distrust.[63]

In its early stages, the university branches of the UJC limited their enrollment to those students of proven Communist militancy. Since 1966, however, they varied their policy and began to actively recruit all students. This change occurred after their candidate lost an election for the presidency of the student association of the Facultad of Technology at the University of Havana to a non-Communist student. These events took place late in 1965. In an assembly of students from the Facultad of Technology two students were nominated for the presidency of the student association. During this assembly, leaders of the UJC brought out a dossier on the life of Juan Manuel Rivero—the candidate they opposed. They accused Rivero of "immoral conduct" and advanced other reasons why he should not be selected. The students, however, selected Rivero by acclamation. Since only one candidate was allowed, when the elections were held UJC attempted to have a write-in vote for their man. They were again unsuccessful and Rivero was elected.[64]

This failure led to the reorganization of the UJC and to a massive purge of students. The UJC held public assemblies accusing groups of students of being "counterrevolutionaries" or "homosexuals." Other students were denounced for failing to volunteer to cut cane, for not serving in the militia, for counterrevolutionary comments in classroom discussions, or for letting their hair grow too long. "From the School of Agriculture alone," explained Fernández Berges, "twenty-five students were expelled." [65] UJC leaders also began a drive to recruit students for the organization. They reasoned that if a majority of students belonged to the UJC, their loyalties and voting behavior could be easily controlled. Since not belonging to the UJC could limit the possibilities for advancement, a large proportion of the student body joined. UJC leaders, however, still are not satisfied with the slow growth of the organization. "The percentage of activists and would-be activists in our organization," explained Crombet, "in relation to the masses whom we must lead and indoctrinate, is minimal, seriously minimal." [66]

Another factor limiting student opposition is the new orientation of university education. In the past, liberal arts studies were emphasized and the universities produced a crop of underemployed intellectuals every year. Today, the emphasis is on technical and scientific studies and the government absorbs almost all university graduates. An assured salaried job and a guaranteed social position after graduation are undoubtedly import disincentives to opposition activity. Since "good behavior" is one of the requisites for government aid, the regime's scholarships have also contributed to political conformism.

This government control over scholarships and future jobs is, however, a double-edged sword. Since the regime makes a considerable investment in educating a student, it will hesitate before stopping his career, especially in its later stages. Students realize and take advantage of their privileged position. In a University of Havana speech, Castro lashed at government-supported technical students "who think they are doing society a favor." "They know," said Fidel, "that technicians are needed and that bourgeois technicians are leaving; therefore, they think they are important." [67]

Then, the class composition of university students has changed. Although statistics are not available, sons of workers and farmers probably constitute a much larger proportion of the student body today than in the past. The regime has started special preparatory courses to qualify industrial workers for university study. Also, students from poor families receive priority attention from the government in the granting of scholarships. This assistance naturally tends to build loyalty to the regime among recipient students.

A final factor is the establishment of the UJC at the universities. Besides its coercive influence, the UJC offers the students a legitimate channel through which they can operate and voice their discontent directly to the party.

These factors indicate that anti-Castro student activity of any significance in the immediate future seems extremely unlikely. The present events in eastern Europe, however, continue to haunt the Cuban government. In challenging the party, the European students and intellectuals are demonstrating the weakness of the system. The experience of Europe is undoubtedly a stern warning to the Cuban Communists.

Opposition to the Communist regime in Cuba does exist, but it has been forced into a passive form. Although anti-Castro slogans are occasionally painted on university walls and government posters at the universities are frequently torn down, opposition is primarily manifested by the students' apathetic attitude toward the regime. This might include refusal to attend government-sponsored meetings and activities, to devote time to "voluntary work," or to conform in general to party directives.[68] These forms of political withdrawal are viewed with extreme concern by party officials, for they represent not only a manifestation of political opposition but also of the government's failure to win the minds of Cuba's youth.

Notes

Chapter 1

1. Cuba, *Gaceta de la Habana* (October 11, 1871), p. 1. After the 1878 Peace of Zanjón, which ended the "Ten Year War," the University was allowed once more the right to grant doctor's degrees. In 1892, however, because of a reduction in expenditures for higher education, the Spanish government again prohibited doctoral studies at the University. For the various educational changes introduced by the Spanish Crown at the University of Havana, see Luis Felipe LeRoy y Gálvez, "El Plan de Estudios de 1863 en la Universidad de la Habana," *Revista de la Universidad de la Habana* (March–June, 1964), pp. 107–149.

2. The arrest and execution of the students has received wide attention among Cuban historians. A narrative of the events can be found, among other places, in Ramiro Guerra y Sánchez *et al., Historia de la Nación Cubana* (La Habana: Editorial Historia de la Nación Cubana, S.A., 1952), V, 139–144.

3. See Gonzalo de Quesada, (ed.), *Obras completas de Martí* (La Habana: Editorial Trópico, 1937), IX, 151–170.

4. "La Conferencia Monetaria," *La Revista Ilustrada* (May, 1891), *ibid.,* XXII, 28. For some of Martí's ideas, see Suchlicki, "The Political Ideology of José Martí," *Caribbean Studies* (April, 1966), pp. 25–36.

5. The Platt Amendment was drafted by the late Senator Orville H. Platt of Connecticut to define the relations between Cuba and the United States after Cuba became independent in 1902. At the insistence of the United States government, the amendment was incorporated in the Cuban Constitution of 1901. According to its Article III, "The government of Cuba consents that the United States may exercise the right to intervene for the preservation of Cuban Independence, the maintenance of a government adequate for the protection of life, property, and individual liberty, and for discharging the obligation with respect to Cuba, imposed by the Treaty of Paris on the United States now to be assumed and undertaken by the government of Cuba." The en-

tire text of the amendment can be found in Samuel Flagg Bemis (ed.), *The American Secretaries of State and Their Diplomacy* (New York: Pageant Book Co., 1958), IX, 386. C. A. M. Hennessy, "The Roots of Cuban Nationalism," *International Affairs,* XXXIX, (London, July, 1963), 350, points out that Cubans blamed United States intervention for frustrating the revolution of 1895 and for diverting Cuban history from the course that Martí had mapped out.

6. Although reorganized after the first United States intervention, the army did not play a prominent political role as a unified body until the 1930's. Two works on the history of Cuba are Guerra y Sánchez *et al., op. cit.,* and Herminio Portell Vilá, *Historia de Cuba,* 4 vols. (La Habana: Editorial Jesús Montero, 1930). This latter study extends only until 1909. Charles E. Chapman, *A History of the Cuban Republic* (New York: The MacMillan Co., 1927) is a fine summary. The relations between Cuba and the United States up to 1895 are described in Philip S. Foner, *A History of Cuba in its Relations with the United States,* 2 vols. (New York: International Publishers, 1963), and in R. H. Fitzgibbon, *Cuba and the United States, 1900–1935* (Wisconsin: Menasha, 1935).

7. Jorge Mañach, "Revolution in Cuba," *Foreign Affairs,* XII (October, 1933), 51. Donald E. Worcester and Wendell G. Schaeffer in *The Growth and Culture of Latin America* (New York: Oxford University Press, 1956), pp. 536–537, attribute the absence of a real sense of responsibility among Latin American countries partly to the fact that under the Spanish administrative system the possession of property did not carry with it either political responsibility or other attributes of European feudalism. Normal A. Bailey, "The U. S. as Caudillo," *Journal of Inter-American Studies* (July, 1963), pp. 313–324, blames the Latin American nations' dependence on the United States on what he calls "the *patrón* mentality," which developed through centuries of feudal economic relations and paternalistic religious concepts.

8. See Alfredo M. Agüayo, "Factores cualitativos de nuestra decadencia escolar," *Revista Bimestre Cubana* (March–April, 1926), pp. 81–95, and Hennessy, *op. cit.,* p. 351.

9. The University of Havana continued to be, until 1947, when the Catholic University Santo Tomás de Villanueva was founded, the only university in Cuba. Later on the government of President Carlos Prío Socarrás established the University of Oriente and the "Marta Abreu" Central University of Las Villas. In addition, several private universities were founded.

10. There were three facultades at the University of Havana: Arts and Sciences, Medicine and Pharmacy, and Law. Of these, Arts and Sciences had 159 students; Medicine and Pharmacy had 338; and Law had 165. See Grupo Cubano de Investigaciones

Económicas, *Un Estudio Sobre Cuba* (Coral Gables: University of Miami Press, 1963), p. 317. See also United States Congress, House, *Annual Reports of the War Department: Report of Enrique José Varona,* 50th Cong., 2nd Sess., 1901, I, 81–95. For a brief history of the University of Havana, see Luis Felipe LeRoy y Gálvez, *La Universidad de La Habana: síntesis histórica* (La Habana: Imprenta de la Universidad, 1960).

11. See Pablo F. Lavín, "El estado cubano y sus problemas educacionales," *Universidad de La Habana,* XXIV (July–December, 1947), 323–331.

12. See Guerra y Sánchez, *op. cit.,* VIII, 59–60.

13. "Mr. Crowder y los estudiantes," *Diario de la Marina,* November 19, 1921, p. 1.

14. For Arce's lecture, see "Solemne acto en la Universidad Nacional," *Diario de la Marina,* December 5, 1922, p. 1, and "Discurso del doctor Arce en la Commemoración del 27 de Noviembre," *ibid.,* December 5, 1922 (evening edition), p. 1. See also "Se suspenderá temporalmente el funcionamiento de la Universidad," *ibid.,* January 16, 1923, p. 1.

15. For the students' manifesto stating their demands, see "Mientras no actúe la Comisión Mixta se considera imposible solucionar el actual problema de la Universidad," *ibid.,* February 9, 1923, p. 1.

16. Interview with Aureliano Sánchez Arango, Miami, Florida, April 15, 1967. Sánchez Arango, as all other persons interviewed, participated actively or was closely connected to the events narrated in this book. Although these interviews provide the main substance to the data obtained, wherever possible documentary evidence has been used to supplement these accounts, i.e., newspapers, magazines, pamphlets, personal letters, tape recorded speeches, and manifestoes. It is obvious that interviews vary in value because of the intense involvement of some and the faulty memories of others. All interviews have, therefore, been used cautiously.

17. The University budget was increased from $260,000 in 1902 to $1,017,000 in 1927. For the reforms that were implemented into the University as a result of the actions of the students, see Eduardo Suárez Rivas, *Un pueblo crucificado* (Coral Gables: Service Offset Printers, 1964), pp. 6–16. Suárez Rivas participated actively in these occurrences and was Vice-President of the Student Federation. See also Luis Felipe LeRoy y Gálvez, "La Universidad de La Habana en su etapa republicana: síntesis histórica," *Revista de la Biblioteca Nacional José Martí* (April–June, 1966), pp. 24–30, and Raúl Roa, "La revolución universitaria de 1923," *Retorno a la alborada* (Las Villas: Universidad de Las Villas, 1964), I, 229–260.

18. In his early years, Mella used the name Nicanor McParland, with which his mother had registered him. Later on, however, he

changed to his father's name. There is no good biography of Mella, only the very eulogistic biographical sketch by Erasmo Dumpierre, *Mella, esbozo biográfico* (La Habana: Instituto de la Historia, 1965). Most of the information was obtained by the author in interviews with Mella's widow, Mrs. Olivín Zaldívar, in Miami, Florida, on April 3, 4, 1967.

19. Julio Antonio Mella, "Los estudiantes y la lucha social," *Ensayos Revolucionarios* (La Habana: Editora Popular de Cuba y del Caribe, 1960). See also *Julio A. Mella: documentos para su vida. Primer Congreso Nacional de Estudiantes* (La Habana: Comisión Nacional Cubana de la UNESCO, 1964).

20. During this period other "popular universities" sprang up throughout Latin America, such as the "Universidad Popular Lastarria" in Chile and the "Universidad Libre" in Buenos Aires.

21. Some of Mella's writings are contained in a small book, *La lucha revolucionaria contra el imperialismo* (La Habana: Editora Popular de Cuba y del Caribe, 1960). See also *Julio A. Mella: documentos para su vida, op. cit.*

22. See Fabio Grobart, "El movimiento obrero cubano de 1925 a 1933," *Cuba Socialista* (August, 1966), pp. 88–120. For a penetrating biographical sketch of Grobart, one of the Party's founders, see Boris Kozolchyk, *The Political Biographies of Three Castro Officials* (Santa Monica: The Rand Corporation, 1966), pp. 1–20.

23. An account of the founding of the Party written by Blas Roca, its Secretary General from 1934 until 1965, can be found in *Hoy,* August 15, 1965 (Sunday Supplement), pp. 2–6.

24. Interview with Rolando Meruelo, Miami, Florida, March 29, 1967. Meruelo, a card carrying member of the Party, broke with the Communists in the 1950's, fleeing to the United States after Castro's revolutionary victory.

25. Dumpierre, *op. cit.,* p. 40.

26. Interview with Mrs. Olivín Zaldívar, *op. cit.*

27. *Ibid.*

Chapter 2

1. The three political parties, Liberal, Conservative, and Popular, nominated Machado as their presidential candidate.

2. "Una refriega frente al Senado entre estudiantes contrarios al proyecto de prórroga de poderes y la policía," *Diario de la Marina,* June 9, 1927, pp. 1, 22.

3. See "Diecisiete jóvenes detenidos en Pinar del Río por alterar el orden y protestar contra la prórroga," *ibid.,* June 21, 1927, p. 1, and "Muchos detenidos en Matanzas," *ibid.*

4. Classes were resumed on June 30. See "Dentro de poco tiempo

se reanudarán las classes en la Universidad Nacional," *ibid.*, June 24, 1927, p. 1, and "El Presidente de la República firmó ayer el decreto de apertura de la Universidad," *ibid.*, June 30, 1927, p. 1.

5. Interview with Aureliano Sánchez Arango, Miami, Florida, April 15, 16, 1967.

6. Among those expelled were Aureliano Sánchez Arango, Eduardo Chibás, Antonio Guiteras, and others. See "Cuarenta y cinco estudiantes serán juzgados en consejo de disciplina por firmar escrito," *Diario de la Marina*, April 14, 1928, p. 1, and Rubén de León, *El Origen del Mal* (Coral Gables: Service Offset Printers, 1964), pp. 291–292. Rubén de León was a prominent leader of the 1930 Directorio.

7. For the "election" results, see "Con orden completo se han efectuado las elecciones . . . con el objeto de votar por la candidatura única," *Diario de la Marina*, November 2, 1928, p. 1.

8. Interview with Aureliano Sánchez Arango, Miami, Florida, April 15, 16, 1967. See also Rubén de León, *op. cit.*, pp. 291–292, and Raúl Roa, *Viento Sur* (La Habana: Editorial Selecta, 1953). Roa, a Directorio activist, narrates in this book some of his student experiences. The members of the Directorio were selected by the students in periodical secret meetings. Usually, for every Directorio member appointed, an alternate was selected. When members of the first Directorio were unable to fulfill their assignment, their positions were automatically occupied by the alternates.

9. For an account by one of the wounded students, see Pablo de la Terriente Brau, *La última sonrisa de Trejo* (La Habana: Delegación del Gobierno en el Capitolio Nacional, 1959). See also "Presentará la renuncia de su cargo de Rector universitario el Dr. Inclán," *Diario de la Marina*, October 1, 1930, p. 1, and "Falleció a las 9:30 el jóven estudiante Trejo," *ibid.*, October 2, 1930, p. 1.

10. See Gerardo Castellanos, *Panorama Histórico: ensayo de cronología cubana* (La Habana: Ucar García y Cía., 1934), p. 1501.

11. "Distinguidas damas y varios estudiantes fueron enviados a la cárcel por hallarse en una casa del Vedado reunidos," *Diario de la Marina*, January 4, 1931, p. 1.

12. "Eighty-five Professors Indicted," *The New York Times*, February 15, 1931, p. 26.

13. See Ricardo Adán y Silva, "Las Conspiraciones en el ejército durante la tiranía," *Bohemia*, August 26, 1934, pp. 50–52, 166–177.

14. Interview with Zoila Mullet, Miami, Florida, March 25, 1967.

15. Interview with Aureliano Sánchez Arango, *op. cit.*

16. *Ibid.*

17. Raúl Roa, "Doce de Agosto," *Retorno a la Alborada* (Las Villas, Universidad de Las Villas, 1964), I, 194–195.

18. Interview with Rolando Meruelo, Miami, Florida, March 29, 1967.
19. *El Partido Comunista y los problemas de la revolución en Cuba* (La Habana: Comité Central del Partido Comunista de Cuba, 1933), p. 11. For the party's strategy during this period, see Paul H. Krauss, *Communist Policy in Cuba* (Columbia University: unpublished Master's thesis, 1950).
20. See *El Partido Comunista y los problemas de la revolución, op. cit.*, pp. 25–26.
21. Interview with Rolando Meruelo, *op. cit.*
22. Interview with Zoila Mullet, *op. cit.*,
23. For the ABC's program see *Doctrina del ABC: Manifiesto-Programa de 1932* (La Habana: Editorial Cénit, 1942).
24. See Eddy Chibás, "Hacia dónde va Cuba," *Bohemia*, August 26, 1934, pp. 63–64.
25. See "Historia de la Revolución," *ibid.*, August 26, 1934, pp. 81–85.
26. A list of those assassinated by the government can be found in *ibid.*, pp. 85–86, 140–149. See also "La muerte de los hermanos Valdés Dausá," *Carteles,* January 14, 1934, p. 20.
27. For the events connected with the United States mediation, see Sumner Welles, *Relations Between the U. S. and Cuba* (Washington, D.C.: Government Printing Office, State Department Latin American Series, No. 7, 1934), and Charles A. Thomson, "The Cuban Revolution: Fall of Machado," *Foreign Policy Reports*, XI, No. 21 (December 18, 1935), 250–260. A good summary of U.S.-Cuban relations during this period can be found in Bryce Wood, *The Making of The Good Neighbor Policy* (New York: W. W. Norton and Company, 1967).
28. "El Gral Menocal explica su actitud frente a la mediación de Mr. Welles," *Diario de la Marina*, July 7, 1933, p. 1.
29. "Havana Students Scorn Mediation," *The New York Times*, July 16, 1933, II, 2. See also Chibás, *op. cit.*, p. 64.
30. Interview with Juan J. Remos, Miami, Florida, April 30, 1965.
31. See Russel B. Porter, "Students Guiding Destinies of Cuba," *The New York Times*, September 15, 1933, p. 6. Porter wrote several other articles favorable to the students. See "Student Idealism Faces Test in Cuba," *ibid.*, September 13, 1933, p. 15, and "Cuba Libre: The New Challenge," *ibid.*, September 17, 1933, VI, pp. 2, 16.
32. Raúl Roa, *Quince Años Después* (La Habana: Selecta, 1950), pp. 408, 561, 579, quoted in Boris Kozolchyk, *The Political Biographies of Three Castro Officials* (Santa Monica: The Rand Corporation, 1966) pp. 29, 32–34.
33. See Kozolchyk, *op. cit.*, pp. 32–34.
34. For the students' program see "Directorio Estudiantil Universitario al Pueblo de Cuba," *Diario de la Marina*, August 24, 1933, p. 1.

35. For an account of the military revolt by a participating army officer, see Horacio Ferrer, "El General Herrera, al traicionar al ejercito precipitó la caída de Machado," *ibid.,* August 23, 1933, p. 4. See also Alberto Lamar Schweyer, *Cómo Cayó el Presidente Machado* (Madrid: Espasa-Calpe, 1934). Schweyer worked as newspaper censor for the Machado regime.

36. Interview with Rolando Meruelo, *op. cit.* Subsequently the Communist-dominated National Confederation of Labor admitted its error, alleging that it had failed to appreciate the true character of the general strike by assuming it to be only economic and not political. See IV Congreso Nacional Obrero de Unidad Sindical, *Resoluciones y acuerdos sobre la estructura orgánica de la CNOC* (La Habana: 1934), p. 11. See also Andrés Suárez, *Cuba: Castroism and Communism, 1959–1966* (Cambridge: M.I.T. Press, 1967). In a preface written in 1936 to Rubén Martínez Villena's book, *La pupila insomne* (La Habana, Editorial Lex, n.d.), Raúl Roa hints that the Communists had reached a modus vivendi with Machado earlier than the time of the general strike.

37. Despite these negative factors, the party grew in membership during the latter part of the 1930's, especially after Grau's frustrated administration. In 1939 party Secretary Francisco Calderío, alias Blas Roca, boasted that the Cuban party had expanded from 2,800 members in January, 1934, to 5,000 by September of that year, and to 23,000 by 1939. He further pointed out that seventy-one percent of the members were workers; twenty-one percent were students, teachers, and small merchants, and eight percent were farmers. See Blas Roca, *Las experiencias de Cuba* (La Habana: Páginas, 1939), pp. 7–8.

38. See "El ABC ante la crisis Cubana," *Diario de la Marina,* September 11, 1933, p. 1.

39. On August 19 one of Machado's most hated henchmen, Chief of Police Antonio Ainciart, shot himself to avoid capture. His naked body was hauled to the University and hung from an electric light pole. See "Antonio B. Ainciart se suicidó anoche, al verse acorralado," *ibid.,* August 20, 1933, p. 1. The Directorio denied any responsibility for these events. See "Aclaración del Directorio de la Universidad," *ibid.,* August 21, 1933, p. 1.

40. "Declaraciones del Directorio Estudiantil Universitario," *ibid.,* August 29, 1933, p. 1.

41. For the students' demands see their manifesto, "Directorio Estudiantil Universitario al Pueblo de Cuba," *ibid.,* August 24, 1933, p. 1.

42. Statement to the Foreign Policy Association by Carlos Prío Socarrás, quoted in Charles A. Thomson, "The Cuban Revolution: Reform and Reaction," *op. cit.,* p. 262.

43. "Destituido el actual gobierno por la Agrupación Revolucionaria

de Cuba," *Diario de la Marina,* September 4, 1933, p. 1. Céspedes did not offer his resignation to the Pentarchy. He finally resigned in January, 1934, just before Mendieta took the oath of office as Provisional President.

44. For the events connected with the rise and fall of the Pentarchy, see José M. Irisarri, "Cómo nació y cómo murió la Comisión Ejecutiva," in *Bohemia,* August 26, 1934, pp. 7, 127–130.

45. *Ibid.,* p. 129.

46. "Fue designado Presidente de la República el Dr. Grau San Martín," *Diario de la Marina,* September 10, 1933, p. 1.

47. Russell B. Porter, "Students Guiding Destinies of Cuba," *The New York Times,* September 15, 1933, p. 6.

48. "Convocada la Convención Nacional Constituyente, que deberá iniciar sus sesiones el 20 de mayo de 1934," *Diario de la Marina,* September 19, 1933, p. 1.

49. Although negotiations began during Grau's regime, abrogation of the Platt Amendment was not secured until 1934 during Mendieta's presidency.

50. The decree 2059, later reaffirmed by the Mendieta government, removed from the Secretary of Education all authority over the University affairs and set aside 2 percent of the national budget for its support. See *Gaceta de la Habana,* October 9, 1933. Despite administrative autonomy, the University remained financially dependent on the government.

51. "Fue firmado el decreto que establece la jornada máxima de ocho horas en toda la República," *Diario de la Marina,* September 20, 1933, p. 1.

52. A discussion of the social and labor legislation implemented during Grau's administration can be found in: Commission on Cuban Affairs, *Problems of the New Cuba* (New York: Foreign Policy Association, 1935), pp. 201–217. See also Ramón Grau San Martín, "El nacionalismo Auténtico y sus leyes," *Bohemia,* August 26, 1934, pp. 125–126.

53. "Mr. Welles se entrevistó anoche con el Directorio Estudiantil Universitario," *Diario de la Marina,* September 16, 1933, p. 1.

54. Chibás, *op. cit.,* p. 64.

55. See Thomson, "The Cuban Revolution: Reform and Reaction," *op. cit.,* p. 265.

56. "Una sangrienta jornada fue la sublevación ocurrida ayer en la Habana," *Diario de la Marina,* November 9, 1933, p. 1. Also see "Tras un intenso bombardeo se rindió ayer el castillo de Atarés," *ibid.,* November 10, 1933, p. 1.

57. Interview with Aureliano Sánchez Arango, *op. cit.*

58. Interviews with Leovigildo Ruiz, Miami, Florida, April 25, 1967, and Aureliano Sánchez Arango, *op. cit.*

59. "Del Directorio Estudiantil al Pueblo de Cuba," *Diario de la Marina,* November 6, 1933, p. 2.

60. See Pablo de la Torriente Brau, "La nueva actitud universitaria,"

Bohemia, January 14, 1934, pp. 32, 41. Torriente Brau, a brave anti-Machado Ala Izquierda leader who had embraced Marxism, died fighting for the Spanish Republic years later. The story of his life is told by his wife, Teresa Casuso, in her book *Cuba and Castro* (New York: Random House, 1961).
61. See Rubén de León, *op. cit.,* pp. 305–307, and "Historia de la Revolución," *Bohemia,* August 26, 1934, pp. 104–105.
62. Ramón Grau San Martín, "The Cuban Terror," *The Nation,* CXL (April 3, 1935), 381.

Chapter 3

1. The PRC became popularly known later on as the Auténticos, a term added on to denote "the genuine revolutionaries." For the events connected with the founding of the party see Rubén de León, *El Origen del Mal* (Coral Gables: Service Offset Printers, 1964), pp. 308–310.
2. "Resultaron lesionados una joven y un vigilante al ser disuelta una manifestación ayer tarde," *Diario de la Marina,* April 15, 1934, p. 1.
3. "Elementos comunistas aprovecharon la coyuntura para promover un grave desorden," *ibid.,* May 4, 1934, p. 1. See also "Arrollada la minoría izquierdista universitaria por el estudiantado sensato," *ibid.,* May 8, 1934, p. 3.
4. For a meeting with Mendieta in which the President handed the students the decree granting university autonomy, see Teresa Casuso, *Cuba and Castro,* (New York: Random House, 1961), pp. 71–72.
5. In the early 1930's the university was organized into three facultades: Arts and Sciences; Medicine and Pharmacy; and Law and Social Sciences.
6. For these events see *Problems of the New Cuba* (New York: Foreign Policy Association, 1935), pp. 150–152.
7. "La Asemblea universitaria acordó retirar su delegación del Frente Único Estudiantil," *Diario de la Marina,* September 13, 1934, p. 2.
8. "Treinta y dos petardos estallaron anoche en la ciudad y sus barrios," *ibid.,* October 1, 1934, p. 1.
9. "Impreciso es el ambiente que existe en la Universidad por el lamentable suceso de ayer," *ibid.,* January 27, 1935, p. 1.
10. "El PRC lanza un manifiesto de pueblo de Cuba sobre la actualidad política nacional," *ibid.,* September 11, 1934, p. 15.
11. See "Mañana volverán a reunirse los componentes del comité de huelga universitario," *ibid.,* February 10, 1935, p. 3, and "Convocado el comité de huelga universitario a una asamblea hoy," *ibid.,* February 13, 1935, p. 2. See also "Se generaliza la huelga en el Magisterio," *ibid.,* February 21, 1935, p. 1.

12. "El Claustro Universitario, por medio de una comisión, propondrá soluciones immediatas," *ibid.,* February 22, 1935, p. 1.
13. "El gobierno es fuerte y tiene resistencia para conjurar el conflicto . . . ," *ibid.,* March 12, 1935, p. 1.
14. The University remained closed until 1937.
15. "La fuerza pública y los amigos de Guiteras combatieron rudamente," *Diario de la Marina,* May 9, 1935, p. 2. For an account of the events connected with Guiteras' death narrated by an eye witness, see Jorge Quintana, "La muerte de Antonio Guiteras," *Bohemia,* September 15, 1946, pp. 30–31, 67, and September 22, 1946, pp. 34–35, 40.
16. John Edwin Fagg, *Cuba, Haiti and the Dominican Republic* (New Jersey: Prentice Hall, 1965), p. 86.
17. For the Batista-Menocal pact see "El general Menocal y Batista departieron . . . sobre el pacto político," *Diario de la Marina,* March 16, 1940, p. 1. See also "Hicieron renuncia de sus cargos el Presidente y Vicepresidente de la convención constituyente," *ibid.,* March 20, 1940, p. 2.
18. A complete record of the debate preceeding the adoption of the Constitution and its text can be found in Andrés M. Lazcano y Mazón, ed., *Constitución de Cuba,* 3 vols. (La Habana: Cultural S.A., 1941). For a summary of the Constitution's main provisions see Wyatt MacGaffey and Clifford R. Barnett, *Twentieth Century Cuba: The Background of the Castro Revolution* (New York: Doubleday & Co., 1965), pp. 129–133.
19. "Manifiesto de la FEU desvirtuando unas acusaciones," *Diario de la Marina,* July 21, 1942, p. 1. Thirteen presidents, one for each student association from the different facultades at the University, formed the FEU and selected the Federation president. Elections were held every year. For the structure of the FEU see José Ramón Rolando Püig y Pupo, *Apuntes sobre la escuela de Derecho y la Universidad de la Habana* (La Habana: Imprenta de la Universidad, 1959).
20. "Ante extraordinaria concurrencia tuvo lugar el mitin de la FEU," *Diario de la Marina,* July 22, 1942, p. 12. Also see "Los comunistas tratan de sembrar el odio, dicen los universitarios," *ibid.,* August 4, 1942, p. 1.
21. "Ante extraordinaria concurrencia tuvo lugar el mitin de la FEU," *ibid.,* July 22, 1942, p. 12.
22. For these events see "Relata el Dr. Chibás que su agresor fue un desconocido," *ibid.,* November 17, 1939, p. 3, and "Siguen la pista de un misterioso automóvil . . . ," *ibid.,* March 2, 1940, p. 1. See also "Busca la policía varios acusados de atentados terroristas," *ibid.,* March 5, 1940, p. 1. There are some who claim that Chibás himself staged this alleged assassination plot to attract public attention.
23. Interview with Aureliano Sánchez Arango, Miami, Florida, April 15, 16, 1967.

24. See "en Cuba," *Bohemia,* September 15, 1946, pp. 42–45.
25. Interview with Aureliano Sánchez Arango, *op. cit.*
26. Interview with L. Ricardo Alonso, Miami, Florida, June 8, 1967. Mr. Alonso was Castro's Ambassador to London until 1965, when he resigned his position.
27. For Tró's interview see Mario G. Del Cueto, "Unión Insurreccional Revolucionaria," *Bohemia,* June 15, 1947, pp. 52–55. Tró's life ended tragically in 1947 in a mass gang fight with MSR leader and head of the Police Bureau of Investigation, Major Mario Salabarría. For Tró's death, see "en Cuba," *ibid.,* September 21, 1947, pp. 51–54, and "Cómo murió Emilio Tró," *ibid.,* pp. 56–61. Masferrer supported Batista's government in the 1950's, fleeing to the United States after Castro's victory in January, 1959.
28. See Boris Kozolchyk, *The Political Biographies of Three Castro Officials* (Santa Monica: The Rand Corporation, 1966), p. 72.
29. Interview with Juan J. Remos, Miami, Florida, April 30, 1965.
30. The University of Havana had its own campus police paid by and under the orders of the University Council. Manolo Castro had murdered his political rival and University of Havana Professor Raúl Fernández Fiallo. See Mario Riera Hernández, *Historial Obrero Cubano* (Miami: Rema Press, 1965), p. 178.
31. "Está al borde de la muerte el líder de la FEU Justo Fuentes," *Diario de la Marina,* April 3, 1949, p. 32.
32. "Resolverán hoy la situación de los 14 estudiantes detenidos," *ibid.,* September 3, 1949, p. 16.
33. For other incidents see William S. Stokes, "National and Local Violence in Cuban Politics," *Southwestern Social Science Quarterly* (September, 1953), pp. 57–63.
34. *El Mundo,* September 5, 1949, p. 3.
35. Interview with Enrique Ovares, Miami, Florida, May 24, 1967. Ovares was president of the FEU in the late 1940's. He participated, together with Fidel Castro and two other Cuban students, in the famous "Bogotazo" of 1948. Ovares supplied the author with most of the information on Fidel's student life. Some information can also be found in Jules Dubois, *Fidel Castro: Rebel-Liberator or Dictator?* (Indianapolis: Bobbs-Merrill, 1959). Also see Gerardo Rodríguez Morejón, *Fidel Castro: Biografía* (La Habana: P. Fernández y Cía., 1959). This very interesting and little known biography was written in the early days of the revolution with information supplied by Castro's mother.
36. Interview with Enrique Ovares, *op. cit.*
37. *Ibid.*
38. Rafael del Pino is in jail in Cuba and Guevara has an important position in the Castro government. Ovares spent several years

in a Castro prison until recently, when he was released and allowed to travel to the United States.

39. Interview with Enrique Ovares, *op. cit.*
40. *Ibid.*
41. *Ibid.* The most determined exponent of the theory that Castro was a Communist since his student days is Nathaniel Weyl. See his *Red Star Over Cuba* (New York: Hillman McFadden, 1961). Mario Lazo, in his book *Dagger in the Heart: American Policy Failures in Cuba* (New York: Funk & Wagnalls, 1968), p. 132, quotes parts of a letter allegedly sent to him by William D. Pawley, then the U.S. Ambassador to Brazil and a delegate to the Bogotá Conference, in which Pawley stated that he heard the following radio broaodcast in Colombia: "This is Fidel Castro from Cuba. This is a Communist revolution. The President has been killed. All the military establishments are in our hands. The Navy has capitulated to us and this revolution has been a success." Pawley made this same allegation before a United States Senate Subcommittee. See. U.S. Congress, Senate, Committee on the Judiciary, *Communist Threat to the U.S. Through the Caribbean*, hearings before a subcommittee of the Committee on the Judiciary, Senate, 86th Congress, 2nd Session, part 10, 1960, pp. 724–725.
42. Senator Pelayo Cuervo charged Grau himself with misappropriations of $174,000,000 during his administration. Also, Dr. Carlos Manuel de la Cruz charged Grau with misappropriating $18,000,000 of the "sugar differential." See William S. Stokes, "The Cuban Revolution and the Presidential Elections of 1948," *Hispanic American Historical Review*, XXXVII, No. 1 (February, 1951), 41–42. Some of the economic and social reforms introduced by the Auténticos are discussed in José Alvarez Díaz, *et. al.*, *Un Estudio Sobre Cuba* (Coral Gables: University of Miami Press, 1963), pp. 783–788.
43. See Stokes, *op. cit.*, pp. 78–79. Writing in 1951, Professor Stokes pointed out that results of the 1948 presidential elections challenged the Auténticos' right to lead the revolution; he questioned the regime's ability to win future electoral contests. See also Carlos González Palacios, *Revolución y seudorrevolución en Cuba* (La Habana: 1948).
44. See Luis Conte Agüero, *Eduardo Chibás, el adalid de Cuba* (Mexico: Editorial Jus, 1955). This very eulogistic biography contains most of Chibás' speeches and writings. In 1950, Mario Llerena, a distinguished Cuban intellectual, called on Chibás to spell out in detail the party's platform as well as to explain the party's policies once it would attain power. See Mario Llerena, "Recado crítico al Senador Chibás," *Bohemia*, July 9, 1950, pp. 31, 112–113. Although the party appointed commissions to draw up a more specific program, little was immediately accomplished. Chibás' death a year later, furthermore, dealt a se-

vere blow to this highly *personalista* party. For Chibás' response to Llerena, see Eduardo Chibás, "Teoría y práctica de un gobierno ortodoxo," *ibid.*, July 16, 1950, pp. 68–69, 90.

Chapter 4

1. "En Cuba," *Bohemia*, December 28, 1952, pp. 67–68.
2. Herbert L. Matthews, "Students in Cuba Opposing Batista," *The New York Times*, April 15, 1952, p. 5.
3. Interview with Alejandro Rodríguez Díaz, Miami, Florida, May 14, 1965.
4. Jorge Mañach, "Discurso de la Escalinata," *Bohemia*, June 1, 1952, p. 52.
5. "En Cuba," *Bohemia*, June 22, 1952, p. 73.
6. Interview with Angel Díaz, Miami, Florida, October 25, 1968.
7. "Resolverá el Tribunal de Urgencia situación de los detenidos," *Diario de la Marina*, April 7, 1953, p. 77 and *Bohemia*, May 31, 1953, pp. 68–69. Bárcena had no program beyond a return to the 1940 Constitution and the holding of free elections.
8. Interview with Angel Díaz, *op. cit.* Some of the students that participated were Castro's brother Raúl, Pedro Miret, and Lester Rodríguez. Hugh Thomas, "Middle Class Politics and the Cuban Revolution" in Claudio Véliz, ed., *The Politics of Conformity in Latin America* (London: Oxford University Press, 1967), p. 260, points out that four University of Havana students dropped out on the morning of the attack.
9. This last point is discussed in Andrés Suárez, *Cuba: Castroism and Communism* (Cambridge: The M.I.T. Press, 1967), p. 20.
10. A number of accounts have been written on the Moncada attack. See Robert Merle, *Moncada: Premier combat de Fidel Castro* (Paris: Robert Laffont, 1965); Robert Taber, *M–26: Biography of a Revolution* (New York: Lyle Stuart, 1961), pp. 32–47; and Jules Dubois, *Fidel Castro: Rebel-Liberator or Dictator* (Indianapolis: Bobbs-Merrill, 1959), pp. 30–83.
11. See "en Cuba," *Bohemia*, October 12, 1952, p. 90; December 14, 1952, p. 73; February 15, 1953, p. 68. See also *Del Consejo Universitario a la opinión pública* (Havana: Imprenta de la Universidad, 1953).
12. *Bohemia*, November 23, 1952, p. 72.
13. *Ibid.*
14. Interview with Alvaro Barba, *Bohemia*, January 4, 1953, pp. 36–37.
15. For a description and photographs of the murdered student's funeral, see *Vida Universitaria*, March, 1953, 13–14. See also Interview with José Joaquín Peláez, *Bohemia*, March 8, 1953, pp. 70–71.
16. "En Cuba," *Bohemia*, May 31, 1953, pp. 68–69.

17. "Celebrado con gran entusiasmo el Primero de Mayo," *Diario de la Marina,* May 2, 1953, p. 1.
18. "En Cuba," *Bohemia,* May 10, 1953, p. 134.
19. Blas Roca, "Las divergencias en cuanto al Programa, los métodos de lucha y la táctica frente a la crisis cubana," *Hoy,* July 19, 1953, quoted in Suárez, *op. cit.,* pp. 19–20.
20. *Ibid.*
21. Interview with Don Cosme de la Torriente, *Bohemia,* October 23, 1955, pp. 86–87.
22. "En Cuba," *Bohemia,* November 20, 1955, pp. 68–69.
23. "Se efectuó la concentración oposicionista en la plazoleta de Luz," *Diario de la Marina,* November 20, 1955, p. 1. See also "en Cuba," *Bohemia,* November 27, 1955, pp. 68–73.
24. Cosme de la Torriente, "Provocó la ruptura la comisión del gobierno," *Bohemia,* March 25, 1956, pp. 56–57. See also *ibid.,* May 6, 1956, p. 51.
25. For these events see "en Cuba," *Bohemia,* January 2, 1955, p. 65; José A. Echeverría, "El canal constituye una agresión directa a nuestra soberanía," *Bohemia,* January 16, 1956, pp. 64–65; and "Forum en la Universidad sobre el canal Vía-Cuba," *Vida Universitaria,* April–May, 1955, p. 23.
26. On these events see *Diario de la Marina,* December 2, 3, 6, and 9, 1955.
27. "En Cuba," *Bohemia,* December 11, 1955, pp. 65–77; December 18, 1955, pp. 127–141, and December 25, 1955, pp. 64–65.
28. *Ibid.,* February 5, 1956, pp. 59–63. Also see "Los sucesos del lunes 13," *ibid.,* February 19, 1956, pp. 56–57.
29. *Ibid.,* February 26, 1956, pp. 76, 84.
30. "En Cuba," *Bohemia,* April 29, 1956, pp. 58–59. Also see "Los trágicos sucesos de Santiago," *ibid.,* pp. 70–71.
31. "En Cuba," *Bohemia,* April 29, 1956, pp. 60–63.
32. See "La violación de la autonomía universitaria: una muestra de incivilidad," *ibid.,* pp. 65–68. The University of Havana remained closed until June 18, 1956.
33. "Reconoce y acata el gobierno la autonomía universitaria," *Diario de la Marina,* April 25, 1956, p. 1.
34. On these events, see "Carta a varios líderes políticos de Cuba," *La sierra y el llano* (Habana: Casa de las Américas, 1961); "La conspiración del 3 de abril," *Bohemia,* April 15, 1956, pp. 63–77; "Cuartel Goicuría, 29 de abril," *Bohemia,* June 10, 1956, pp. 60–65. The *Organización Auténtica* was an insurrectionary offshoot of the Auténtico party.
35. Interview with Armando Fleites, Miami, Florida, July 12, 1965. For the students' demands see *Bohemia,* December 4, 1955, p. 74. Of the eight original founders of the Directorio, José A. Echeverría, Fructuoso Rodríguez, Joe Westbrook, and Tirso Urdanivia died in the struggle against Batista, Faure Chomón and René Anillo are in Cuba supporting the revolutionary re-

gime, René Valls is in jail in Cuba, and Félix Armando Murias is in exile.

36. Interview with Félix Armando Murias, Miami, Florida, July 19, 1965.
37. Interview with Armando Fleites, Miami, Florida, July 12, 1965.
38. Interview with Félix Armando Murias, *op. cit.*
39. *Ibid.* The Directorio Revolucionario Estudiantil, a former anti-Castro student organization in exile, provided the author with a copy of "La Carta de México."
40. "La muerte del Coronel Blanco Rico," *Diario de la Marina,* October 27, 1956, p. 1. Also see "La trágica muerte del Coronel Blanco Rico," *Bohemia,* November 4, 1956, pp. 60–66. Carbó Serviá sought refuge in a Latin American embassy and Cubela escaped to Miami.
41. Interview with Fidel Castro in México, *Bohemia,* January 6, 1957, p. 6.
42. Interview with Félix Armando Murias, *op. cit.* Similar statements, claiming that Fidel failed to notify the Directorio in advance of his landing, were made in other interviews by Juan A. Rodríguez, Miami, May 7, 1965; Annaelis Esteva, Miami, May 11, 1965; and Armando Fleites, Miami, July 12, 1965.
43. Several years later, Directorio leader Faure Chomón, justifying the students' inaction, said that at the time the students lacked "the necessary means" (i.e., weapons) to stage a revolt in Havana. Testimony of Faure Chomón at the trial of Marco Armando Rodríguez, *Hoy,* March 24, 1964, p. 8.
44. "Suspenden clases en la Universidad," *Diario de la Marina,* December 1, 1956, p. 1; December 3, 1956, p. 1. Also see "Calmada la capital de Oriente después de dos jornadas de sucesos," *ibid.,* December 2, 1956, p. 1.
45. Interview with former FEU leader Juan A. Rodríguez, *op. cit.*
46. Interview with Armando Fleites, Miami, *op. cit.* See also "Hicieron explosión ocho petardos en La Habana," *Diario de la Marina,* January 1, 1957, p. 1.
47. The events that preceded the attack on the palace and the attack itself are narrated by one of the participants, Faure Chomón, in a series of three articles entitled "El ataque al palacio presidencial el 13 de marzo de 1957," *Bohemia,* March 15, 1959; March 22, 1959 and April 5, 1959.
48. These were Faure Chomón, Víctor Bravo, and José Luis Gómez Wangüemert.
49. Herbert L. Matthews, "Old Order in Cuba Is Threatened by Forces of an Internal Revolt," *The New York Times,* February 26, 1957, p. 13.
50. Herbert L. Matthews, *The Cuban Story* (New York: George Braziller, 1961) p. 43.
51. Faure Chomón, "El ataque al Palacio Presidencial," *Bohemia,* March 22, 1959, p. 72.

52. The strategy for the assault on the Presidential Palace was explained by Eloy Gutiérrez Menoyo, brother of the military leader of the attack, in an interview for *Bohemia*, February 1, 1959.

53. *Ibid.*

54. Chomón, *op. cit.*, p. 73. See also: Julio García Olivera, "La operación Radio Reloj," *Bohemia*, March 15, 1959, pp. 10–12. García Olivera was in charge of the military take-over of the broadcasting station.

55. Chomón, *op cit.*, p. 73.

56. "El aporte del Directorio Revolucionario en la lucha contra la tiranía," *Bohemia*, January 11, 1959, pp. 56–59.

57. *Ibid.*

58. *Ibid.*

59. Faure Chomón, "El ataque al Palacio Presidencial," *La sierra y el llano*, (La Habana: Casa de las Américas, 1961), p. 108.

60. "Frustrado el asalto al Palacio Presidencial por un grupo de 40 hombres con numerosas armas," *Diario de la Marina*, March 14, 1957, p. 12A.

61. *Ibid.*

62. Robert Taber, *op. cit.*, pp. 114–115.

63. *Ibid.*, p. 116.

64. "Rebel Suicide Squad Wiped Out," *The Times of Havana*, March 14, 1957, p. 41.

65. Taber, *op cit.*, p. 117.

66. *Ibid.*, p. 118.

67. On these events see Julio García Olivera, *op. cit.*, pp. 10–12.

68. "En Cuba," *Bohemia*, May 28, 1957, p. 97.

69. The text of Marinello's letter can be found in Herbert L. Mathews, *The Cuban Story* (New York: George Braziller, 1961), pp. 51–52. See also Theodore Draper, *Castroism, Theory and Practice* (New York: Praeger, 1965), pp. 30–31.

70. Testimony of Raúl Valdés Vivó at the trial of Marco Armando Rodríguez, *Hoy*, March 25, 1964, p. 4.

71. Later, in February, 1957, in a letter to the 26th of July Movement, the PSP leaders also called on Castro for "closer understanding" based on a "coincidence" of strategy. They insisted that armed action was the wrong tactic and repeated their disagreement with Fidel's "methods and tactics." They noted, however, that among the different groups in Cuba the 26th of July Movement "came closest" to the Communists' "stategic conception." "Carta del Comité Nacional del Partido Socialista Popular al Movimiento 26 de julio," February 28, 1957, quoted in Draper, *Castroism*, pp. 29–30.

72. Interview with Dora Rosales, Miami, June 14, 1965. Mrs. (Rosales) Westbrook, Joe Westbrook's mother, took up the fight against Batista after her son's death. She went into exile and traveled throughout Latin America denouncing Batista. After

Castro came to power, she returned to Cuba and supported the revolutionary regime. When it became clear to her that communism had gained control in Cuba, she again went into exile and denounced the Castro regime.

73. After Castro's victory, it was established that Marco Armando Rodríguez ("Marquito"), a Communist informer, had denounced the students to Batista's police.

74. "Woman's Brief Reign Ends as President of the FEU," *The Times of Havana*, April 25, 1957, p. 3.

75. A tape recording of Chomón's original speech was supplied to the author by Ada Azcarreta in Miami, May 7, 1965.

76. For Castro's manifesto, see Gregorio Selser, ed., *La Revolución Cubana* (Buenos Aires: Editorial Palestra, 1960), pp. 119–126.

77. For the full text of the letter, see *ibid.*, pp. 127–140.

78. *Revolución*, December 1, 1961.

79. See "Declaraciones del PSP: Las mentiras del Gobierno sobre la huelga y la situación," PSP leaflet of April 12, 1968, quoted in Draper, *op. cit.*, p. 32. In a speech at the cultural society Nuestro Tiempo (a front organization of the PSP) in January, 1959, Che Guevara discussed the strike and the ideological struggle within the 26th of July Movement. Guevara's speech can be found in Selser, *op. cit.*, pp. 427–436.

80. Fleites interview, *op. cit.* Fleites reported that when a PSP representative, Ovidio Díaz, visited his headquarters in the mountains in August, 1958, to propose unity, "he [Díaz] met with our stern opposition to any pacts with the Communists."

81. Dr. Manuel Urrutia, a distinguished judge, was accepted as head of the provisional government to be established after Batista's overthrow. The "Caracas Letter" of July 28, 1958, called for: a common strategy of armed insurrection, a brief provisional government that would guide the country back to normality through constitutional and democratic means, and a minimum government program guaranteeing the punishment of the guilty, workers' rights, order, peace, freedom, the fulfillment of international agreements, and the economic, social, and institutional progress of the Cuba people. For the full text, see Selser, *op. cit.*, pp. 152–155.

82. Draper claims (*op. cit.*, pp. 32–34), that Castro surreptitiously negotiated a separate unity pact with the Communists in 1958.

83. Interview with Lázaro Fariñas, Miami, July 2, 1965. Fariñas, a Directorio member, fought under Cubela in the Escambray Mountains. See also Faure Chomón, "Cuando el Che llegó al Escambray," *Bohemia*, December 10, 1965, pp. 52–56. The guerrilla forces of the Directorio signed in November, 1958, a unity pact known as "Pacto del Pedrero" with the invasion forces of the 26th of July Movement that arrived in Las Villas province led by Che Guevara. See *13 documentos de la insurrección* (La Habana: Organización Nacional de Bibliotecas ambulantes y populares, 1959), pp. 63–64.

Chapter 5

1. Interview with Jorge Nóbrega, Miami, Florida, September 12, 1966.
2. "Hará el gobierno justicia serena pero muy enérgica," *Revolución,* January 7, 1959, p. 5.
3. "Armas para qué?," *Revolución,* January 9, 1959, p. 1.
4. "Resolverá el gobierno," *Revolución,* January 10, 1959, p. 1.
5. Chomón described his role in these terms: "When in 1959 the 26th of July Movement, the PSP, and the Directorio worked jointly to decide the true course of the Revolution . . . we organized the so-called left among the insurrectionary groups to defeat the right." Testimony of Faure Chomón at the trial of Marco Armando Rodríguez, *Hoy,* March 21, 1964, p. 5.
6. The tribunals were composed of three professors and two students. Similar procedures were followed at the two other universities. See "Comisión Mixta para la depuración universitaria," *Revolución,* March 25, 1959, p. 1. For the Commission's reform plans, see *Acuerdos de la Comisión Mixta de Reforma Universitaria* (La Habana: Imprenta de la Universidad, 1959).
7. Interview with Jorge Nóbrega, *op. cit.* Also see Luis Boza, *La situación universitaria en Cuba* (Santiago de Chile: Editorial del Pacífico, 1962), p. 24. For the government's version of events surrounding the 1959 election, see *La Universidad de La Habana al Consejo Ejecutivo y a la Asamblea General de la Unión de Universidades de América Latina* (La Habana: Universidad de La Habana, 1964), pp. 44–50.
8. As has already been noted, the assassination of Blanco Rico in 1956—in which Cubela took part—met with considerable indignation in Cuba and was criticized by Castro in Mexico. According to the Directorio's representative in Miami at the time, this censure disturbed Cubela so deeply that, after escaping to the United States, he underwent psychiatric treatment. (Interview with Ada Azcarreta, Miami, May 7, 1965.) In interviews with the author, Jorge Nóbrega, Juan A. Rodríguez, and several other student activists who knew Cubela well portrayed him as unstable and easily influenced.
9. Boitel belonged to the 26th of July Movement underground in Havana. Prior to Castro's December, 1956, landing in Cuba, sporadic cells had been organized throughout the island, one of them among University of Havana students. This underground, a part of the 26th of July Movement, grew in size and importance after the ill-fated attack on the Presidential Palace in March, 1957. Although students joined both the underground and the guerrilla forces, the 26th of July Movement never included a substantial student participation. During the insurrection, the Communists were never able to infiltrate the underground to the degree they did the guerrilla forces.
10. Juan Miguel Portuondo de Castro, *Cómo se apoderaron los co-*

munistas de la Universidad de La Habana (Florida: Directorio Magisterial Cubano, 1962), p. 21. Dr. Portuondo, a distinguished Cuban physician, was at the time Professor of Physiology at the University of Havana. See also *La destrucción de la enseñanza universitaria* (Florida: Directorio Magisterial Cubano, n.d.), p. 13.

11. Boza, *op. cit.*, pp. 29–30. For Castro's statements, see "Declaraciones de Fidel Castro," *Revolución,* October 17, 1959, p. 1.

12. *Ibid.,* p. 31. When the University reopened in 1959, the old system of indirect election for the FEU president had been changed and students were allowed to vote directly for candidates.

13. See "Directed Democracy for FEU," *Youth and Freedom,* VII No. 2 (1965), 16, and "Reestructurarán las dirigencias de la FEU y la UJC," *Vida Universitaria* (April–May, 1966), pp. 6–8. Crombet became the Secretary General of the Union of Young Communists (Unión de Jóvenes Comunistas). Dorticós was the nephew of Cuba's President, Osvaldo Dorticós.

14. Former FEU Vice-President Enrique Velazco, with 7,771 votes to medical student Juan Vila's 7,544, became President of the FEU "Daily News from the Cuban Radio" (USIA, Miami, December 7, 1966), p. 6. See also "New officers for FEU and UJC," *Youth and Freedom,* IX, Nos. 1–2 (1967), 30.

15. "Pide el Consejo Universitario al gobierno actúe en su crisis," *Revolución,* October 8, 1959, p. 1.

16. "Una sola reforma para las 3 universidades oficiales," *ibid.,* April 6, 1960, pp. 1, 6. Also see "Universidades," *ibid.,* April 11, 1960, p. 18.

17. "Piden un consejo de Enseñanza Superior," *ibid.,* April 21, 1960, p. 2; "Comisión coordinadora para las Universidades," *ibid.,* May 5, 1960, p. 7.

18. See *ibid.,* June 17, 1960, p. 7. Also "Expulsará la Universidad a Aureliano Sánchez Arango," *ibid.,* June 20, 1960, p. 1.

19. See Portuondo de Castro, *op. cit.,* pp. 48–49. On the events described, see *ibid.,* p. 43; "Rechaza la FEU la actitud del Consejo Universitario," *Revolución,* June 29, 1960, p. 2; "Acusa la FEU al Consejo," *ibid.,* July 2, 1960, p. 1; "Constituida la Junta Superior de Gobierno de la Universidad," *ibid.,* July 16, 1960, p. 1. Also see Pedro Vicente Aja, "La crisis de la Universidad de La Habana," *Ensayos* (Quito), August, 1962, pp. 39–46.

20. *La reforma de la Enseñanza Superior en Cuba* (Havana: Consejo Superior de Universidades, 1962), p. 14. This monograph describes the new structure of Cuba's three state universities. For other educational changes, see U.S. Office of Education, Division of International Studies, *Educational Data: Cuba* (Washington, D.C.: Government Printing Office, November, 1962); Richard R. Fagen, *Cuba: The Political Content of Adult Education* (Stanford, California: Stanford University, The Hoover Institution on War, Revolution and Peace, 1964); and Joseph S. Roucek, "Pro-Communist Revolution in Cuban Education,"

Journal of Inter-American Studies, VI, 3 (July, 1964), 325–335.

21. Interview with Luis Fernández Rocha, a prominent student leader in Havana at the time and later coordinator of the anti-Castro Revolutionary Student Directorate (DRE) in exile, Miami, September 18, 1966.
22. Boza, *op. cit.,* pp. 180–185. Also see *La Reforma de la Enseñanza Superior en Cuba, op. cit.*
23. For Max Frankel's interview with Carlos Rafael Rodríguez, see *The New York Times,* November 27, 1960, p. 1.
24. *Ibid.,* January 11, 1962, p. 1.
25. The most important cases were the dismissal of the first President, Dr. Manuel Urrutia, in July, 1959; the arrest of Major Huber Matos, commander of the Rebel Army in Camagüey Province, in October; and the removal of two ministers, Faustino Pérez and Manolo Ray, in November.
26. Some of the more important were Rescate, the Triple A, the Revolutionary Recovery Movement (MRR), and the Christian Democratic Party.
27. Interview with Juan Manuel Salvat, Miami, September 14, 1966. The Trinchera group drew its name from one of Martí's maxims: "Trenches of ideas are stronger than trenches of stone."
28. Salvat interview; interview with Juan A. Rodríguez, Miami, September 17, 1966; "Saludo a Anastas Mikoyan," *Revolución,* February 6, 1960, pp. 1, 16; "Chiflaron a Conte Agüero," *ibid.,* March 26, 1960, p. 1. Early in 1960, the FEU organized student militias within the University of Havana. Only FEU leaders and students of "revolutionary militancy" were allowed to join.
29. Salvat, *op. cit.* Artime was later closely involved in the ill-fated invasion attempt at the Bay of Pigs.
30. "Respaldo a la FEU," *Revolución,* March 28, 1960, p. 1. See also "Instauran tribunal para universitarios," *ibid.,* February 6, 1960, p. 4.
31. "Plan," *ibid.,* March 31, 1960, p. 1.
32. Interview with Manuel Artime, Miami, Florida, August 3, 1968.
33. "In its beginning," said Salvat, "the DRE had only 100 student members. But by 1961 it had grown into a clandestine army of 1,800 in Havana alone," (Salvat interview.) These figures cannot, of course, be verified.
34. *La cruz sigue en pie* (Caracas: Directorio Revolucionario Estudiantil, n.d.), p. 35. This pamphlet contains a short biography of Müller and a collection of his writings.
35. *Ibid.,* pp. 21, 28–29.
36. "Cumplidas las sentencias a alzados del Escambray," *Revolución,* October 13, 1960, p. 1.
37. Rocha and Salvat interviews.
38. Rocha interview.
39. Virgilio Campanería, law student, and Alberto Tapia Ruano, architecture student, for example, were executed on April 18, 1961. A list of students executed or jailed can be found in Boza, *op. cit.,* pp. 189–199.

40. Later, while on a trip to East Germany, Medina defected from the Castro regime.
41. According to Salvat, there are a few DRE activists still in Cuba, but "their activities are very limited. They don't know whom they can trust." (Salvat interview.)
42. "Crearán una organización de toda la juventud cubana," *Revolución,* October 24, 1960, p. 1.
43. "Tomó la AJR el nombre de Unión de Jóvenes Comunistas," *Hoy,* April 1, 1962, p. 1. Also see Jaime Crombet, "La UJC en la Universidad de La Habana," *Vida Universitaria,* March, 1964, pp. 10–12. By December, 1966, the UJC University Bureau had a membership of 1,902 students. See "UJC-Comité Universitario," *ibid.,* December, 1966, p. 39.
44. "Daily News from the Cuban Radio," (USIA, Miami), November 21, 1967, p. 2.
45. In June, 1965, Salvador Vilaseca, President of Cuba's National Bank, became the new Rector. See "Nuevo Rector universitario," *ibid.,* August, 1965, pp. 4–6.
46. "La Revolución no ha de ser ni tolerante ni implacable," *Hoy,* March 27, 1964, p. 6. The full text of the trial was published, among other places, in *Hoy, March 24–27, 1964. Hoy* was the official PSP newspaper, it merged with *Revolución* in 1966 to form *Granma,* the present official newspaper of Cuba's Communist Party.
47. On the Marquito affair also see *Humboldt y el Comunismo cubano* (Panamá: Directorio Revolucionario Estudiantil, n.d.) and Janette Habel, "Le Procès de Marcos Rodríguez et les Problèmes de l'unité du Mouvement Revolutionnaire à Cuba," *Les Temps Modernes,* No. 219–220 (September, 1964), 491–531.
48. Only a few months after the trial Joaquín Ordoqui was arrested and accused of "political crimes." His wife, Edith García Buchaca, was relieved of her post at the National Council of Culture. On February 15, 1965, Fidel purged Carlos Rafael Rodríguez as Director of the INRA and appointed himself to that position. Other old PSP leaders were scorned and attacked by Castro's press.
49. "Ordenó Castro que no se aplique la pena de muerte a Cubela," *Diario Las Américas,* March 10, 1966, p. 1. See also the "Proceedings of the Trial of CIA agents which took place at La Cabaña Fortress in Havana and started on 7 March, 1966," *Cuban Embassy Information Bulletin* (London), No. 8 (1966). In interviews with the author, Edgar Sopo, one of Artime's top lieutenants and a prominent MRR member, reported that Cubela had been conspiring within Cuba's armed forces since 1961. According to Sopo, while attending a student congress in Europe early in 1965, Cubela met with Artime in Spain, where they drew up plans to kill Castro. Artime left immediately for Central America and Cubela returned to Cuba to prepare the assassination attempt. The MRR supplied Cubela with the mur-

der weapon, a high-powered telescopic rifle. (Interviews with Edgar Sopo, Miami, September 21 and 23, 1966.)

50. See preceding note. Also see "Fue tomada militarmente la Universidad de La Habana," *ibid.,* March 18, 1966, p. 9.

51. See *The New York Times,* June 15, 1965, p. 12, and "Nuevo núcleo del PCC en la universidad," *Vida Universitaria,* March, 1966, pp. 16–17.

52. For Hart's speech discussing the operation of the Communist Party of Cuba at the universities see *Granma,* December 18, 1967.

Chapter 6

1. Armando Hart, "Objetivos de la educación secundaria en Cuba," *Boletín de la Universidad de Chile* (June, 1965), p. 26.

2. *Hoy,* June 24, 1965, p. 6.

3. For this very interesting speech in which Fidel described some of his regime's educational objectives, see *Granma,* February 5, 1967. See also Miguel Rodríguez, "El entrenamiento del hombre nuevo," *Juventud Rebelde,* October 15, 1966, p. 3. This is the first of four articles published by *Juventud Rebelde* dealing with the development and training of Cuba's youth.

4. *Granma,* December 17, 1967, p. 3.

5. See Lee Lockwood's interview with Fidel published in *Playboy,* January, 1967, p. 79.

6. *Granma,* May 19, 1967.

7. *Granma Weekly Review,* March 3, 1968, p. 5.

8. *The Miami News,* August 4, 1967. For a fine discussion of Cuban propaganda against the United States see Richard R. Fagen, "Mass Mobilization in Cuba: The Symbolism of Struggle," *Journal of International Affairs,* No. 20 (1966), 254–271.

9. See Richard R. Fagen, "The Cuban Revolution: Enemies and Friends," in David J. Finlay, *et. al., Enemies in Politics* (Chicago: Rand McNally and Company, 1967), pp. 226–227.

10. *Granma,* July 27, 1967.

11. Edith García Buchaca, "Las transformaciones culturales de la revolución cubana," *Cuba Socialista,* No. 29 (January, 1964), 47–48.

12. José A. Portuondo, "Los intelectuales y la Revolución," *ibid.,* No. 34 (June, 1964), 62–63 (italics in the original text).

13. A list of books published in Spanish by the Government's Publishing House includes the following: Lenin, *Complete Works,* 29 vols.; Marx and Engels, *Selected Works,* 3 vols.; Kelly and Kovalzon, *Forms of Social Conscience;* G. Cogniot, *Religion and Science;* V. Perlo, *The Empire of High Finance and United States Imperialism;* Mao Tse-tung, *On Ways of Resolving Contradictions Within the People;* A. Kahn, *Scandal in the United States;* V. Afanasyest, *Fundamentals of Philosophical Knowledge;* L. I. Gurvich, *The Role of Natural Wealth in the Devel-*

opment of Productive Forces; Vo Nguyen Giap, *People's War —People's Army;* V. D. Sokolovsky, *Military Strategy.* For a more complete list see Ladislao G. Carvajal, "Sin libros no hay conciencia, no hay comunismo," *Cuba Socialista,* No. 31 (March, 1964), 42–52.

14. See Ernesto Che Guevara, *Man and Socialism in Cuba* (Havana: Book Institute, 1967), pp. 20, 24–25.

15. By 1962 enrollment at the University of Havana had dwindled to 13,430 students. See Dudley Seers, ed., *Cuba: The Economic and Social Revolution* (Chapel Hill: The University of North Carolina Press, 1964), pp. 255–256. At the beginning of the 1966–1967 academic year there were 20,029 students enrolled at the University of Havana, 4,264 at Las Villas University, and 5,246 at Oriente University. See *Cuba 1967, The Educational Movement* (Havana: Ministry of Education, 1967). This pamphlet contains the Cuban's government's report to the XXX International Conference on Public Instruction convoked by the OIE and the UNESCO and held in Geneva, July 6–15, 1967. For the 1967–68 academic year, enrollment at the University of Havana had increased to 21,009 students. There were 1,341 students in the Facultad of Humanities; 2,413 in Sciences; 5,455 in Technology; 1,286 in Agriculture-Livestock; 4,383 in Medicine; 1,190 in the Institute of Economics; 4,695 in the Pedagogic Institute; and 246 non-degree students. These figures have been supplied through the courtesy of Dr. Emilio Peña Fernández, Director of Public Relations at the University of Havana.

16. *Granma,* December 18, 1967, p. 1.

17. Interview with Salvador Vilaseca, *Bohemia,* July 22, 1966, pp. 30–34.

18. *La Reforma de la Enseñanza Superior en Cuba* (La Habana: Consejo Superior de Universidades, 1962). The Plan, which was published in the Official Gazette, became effective on January 10, 1962.

19. *Hoy,* June 24, 1965, p. 6.

20. Armando Hart, "La enseñanza técnica y profesional de nivel medio y universitario," *Cuba Socialista,* No. 33 (May, 1964), 38.

21. Oscar F. Rego, "Plan de organización para las tres universidades," *Vida Universitaria,* No. 186 (February, 1966), 24–25.

22. There are at the University of Havana five Facultades: Humanities, Sciences, Technology, Agricultural-Livestock Sciences, and Medical Sciences. The Facultad of Humanities has four schools: Letters and Arts, History, Legal Sciences, and Political Sciences. Formerly, History did not rate a school of its own, but because of its strategic importance in Marxist education, it has now been promoted to higher organizational status. The opposite happened to Philosophy, which prior to the revolution rated as a school and now has been demoted to a department rank. The government justifies the change explaining that there are not sufficient numbers of intellectuals with Marxist formation who could be professors of Philosophy. See Luis Rolando Cabrera

"La formación de profesionales en las universidades cubanas," *El Siglo Veinte* (Mexico), No. 64 (March, 1966), 29–30. Sciences has seven schools: Mathematics, Physics, Chemistry, Biological Sciences, Pharmaceutical Biochemistry, Geography, and Psychology. In the other two universities there are only the schools of Mathematics, Chemistry, and Psychology. Technology has seven schools: Civil Engineering, Electrical Engineering, Mechanical Engineering, Chemical Engineering, Industrial Engineering, Architecture, and Basic Sciences. The University of Oriente offers in addition a special course of studies leading to the degree of Engineer in Geology. Agriculture-Livestock Sciences has two schools: Agronomy Engineering and Veterinary Medicine. This Facultad does not exist at Oriente or Las Villas University. Medical Sciences has also two schools: Medicine and Dentistry. There is also the Worker-Farmer Preparatory Faculty, the Pedagogic Institute, and the Institute of Economics. The University of Las Villas has four Facultades: Humanities, Technology, Science, and Agricultural-Livestock Sciences. The University of Oriente has four Facultades: Technology, Humanities, Sciences, and Medical Sciences, the Institute of Economics, and the Frank País Pedagogical Institute. The University of Las Villas has announced the opening of a School of Medicine.

23. Carlos Rafael Rodríguez, "La Reforma universitaria," *Cuba Socialista,* No. 6 (February, 1962), 36–37.

24. Interview with Salvador Vilaseca, *Bohemia,* July 22, 1966, pp. 30–34.

25. Carlos Rafael Rodríguez, *op. cit.,* pp. 41–42.

26. See Heinz Hartman, "Sociology in Cuba," *American Sociological Review,* Vol. 28 (August, 1963), 624–628. The new school numbers four departments: Political Theory, Political and Social Problems, Diplomacy, and Administration.

27. See J. B. Moré Benítez, "La revolución técnica y la escuela universitaria de Ciencias Políticas," *Cuba Socialista,* No. 37 (September, 1964), 64–77. See also Euclides Vázquez Candela, "La nueva escuela de Ciencias Políticas," *Revolución,* November 9, 1964, pp. 1–2.

28. See "Universidad: La Escuela de Economía," *Bohemia,* May 29, 1964, pp. 67, 74. The School was divided into the departments of Political Economics, Accounting, and Planning. Courses offered include Political Economy of Capitalism, Political Economy of Socialism, Economic History, Industrial Economics, Agrarian Economics, History of Economic Thought, and Scientific Communism. There are four areas of specialization for the student of Economics: Political Economy, Planning and Statistics, Agrarian Economics, and Industrial Economics. The areas of specialization for Public Accountant are not clearly defined but they include courses in Cost Accounting, Management of Enterprises, and Organizations and Systems.

29. Carlos Rafael Rodríguez, *op. cit.*, p. 34.
30. Armando Hart, "La enseñanza técnica y profesional de nivel medio y universitario," *Cuba Socialista*, No. 33 (May, 1964), 39–40.
31. Parts of the polemic have been reported by an Italian writer, Saverio Tutino, in an article in the theoretical organ of the Italian Communist Party, *Rinascita*, Vol. 23, No. 52 (December 31, 1966), 17–18. See also Humberto Pérez and Félix de la Luz "Contribución a un diálogo," *Teoría y Práctica*, No. 31 (October, 1966), 1–9. These two EIR instructors defended the manuals and emphasized the need to have a simplified version of Marxism-Leninism synthesized in a manual to make it available to "the less sophisticated masses."
32. See *Granma*, February 7, 1967.
33. Ricardo Alarcón is a good example of a student leader emerging out of the UJC–FEU ranks to become the Cuban delegate to the United Nations.
34. Hart defined the intermediate technician as the one who directed the production process as distinguished from the skilled worker who labored with his hands and the university-trained engineer who planned the production process. See Armando Hart, "La enseñanza técnica y profesional de nivel medio y universitario," *Cuba Socialista*, No. 33 (May, 1964), 25–41. There were at the beginning of the 1966–67 academic year 3,017 faculty members at the University of Havana, 573 at Las Villas University, and 656 at Oriente University. See *Cuba 1967, Educational Development* (Havana: Ministry of Education, 1967).
35. Interview with Luis Fernández Berges, Miami, Florida, October 19, 1967. In 1968 several western European scientists offered courses and worked in research at the University of Havana. Among these were K. Krickeberg of the University of Heidelberg, D. Dacunka Castelle of Strasbourg University, Ruben Binaghi of the College de France, and Mario Luzzati of the Center of Molecular Genetics at Gifsur-Ivette in Paris. See *Granma Weekly Review*, September 15, 1968, p. 4.
36. Oscar F. Rego, "Dos profesores de Historia de la Universidad de La Habana en la Universidad de Lomonosov de Moscú," *Vida Universitaria*, No. 199 (March, 1967), 12–13.
37. See *Sierra Maestra* (Santiago de Cuba), August 10, 1966, p. 2.
38. See Oscar F. Rego, "Plan de organización para las tres universidades," *Vida Universitaria*, No. 168 (February, 1966), 24–25. Those taking the course continue to receive their salaries.
39. Interview with Delfín González, Miami, Florida, October 13, 1967. Mr. González, an elementary school teacher since 1950, was fired from his job in 1965 when he applied to leave Cuba.
40. See George S. Counts, *The Challenge of Soviet Education* (New York: McGraw-Hill, 1957), 145–146.
41. The number of scholarships has increased continuously. Up to 1964 there were 6,967 students holding scholarships in the three

universities (approximately 25% of the total number of students). The University of Havana had by far the largest number of scholarship holders, 4,881, while Las Villas had 1,034 and Oriente 1,052. In 1966 there were 7,565 students holding scholarships at the University of Havana alone. See Oscar F. Rego, "Educación en Cuba," *Siglo Veinte* (Mexico) No. 63, (February, 1966), 13, 40. According to data furnished by the Cuban Ministry of Education, the government is investing annually over one thousand pesos in each scholarship holder.

42. *Ibid.*
43. Unmarried students receive 50 pesos a month; married, 90 pesos; married with one dependent, 130 pesos; married with more than two dependents, 150 pesos. See *Juventud Rebelde,* November 24, 1965, p. 5.
44. Interview with Luis Fernández Berges, *op. cit.* In September, 1964, Sergei Sakhin, Chief of the Department of Foreign Students of the Ministry of Secondary and Specialized Education of the USSR, revealed that Cuba was among the countries that had sent the greatest number of students that year to the highly specialized centers of education of the USSR. That number was placed at 315. See *Hoy,* September, 1964, p. 3. The total number of scholarship students in foreign countries in 1967 was placed at 1,815.
45. Marta Vignier, "La Universidad de La Habana," *Siglo Veinte* (Mexico), No. 63 (February, 1966), 22–23.
46. *Juventud Rebelde,* February 8, 1966, p. 1.
47. See Lee Lockwood, *Castro's Cuba, Cuba's Fidel* (New York: The McMillian Co., 1967), p. 125.
48. See *Juventud Rebelde,* August 17, 1966, p. 4.
49. There are five such academies belonging to the FAR: the Aviation Cadet School, the Naval Academy, the Military Technical Institute, the Artillery Cadet School, and the Inter-Service Cadet School.
50. *Granma,* March 30, 1967, p. 6.
51. *Sierra Maestra,* May 12, 1966, p. 1. See also "Estudiantes universitarios estudian medicina militar," *Juventud Rebelde,* February 23, 1966, p. 8.
52. For Crombet's address see *Juventud Rebelde,* March 3, 1966, p. 4 and March 4, 1966, pp. 4, 7.
53. The Soviet *rabfac* or workers faculty originated in Moscow in 1919 and developed into a major educational institution in the 1920's. With the growth of primary and secondary education it lost importance in the 1940's. See George S. Counts, *The Challenge of Soviet Education,* pp. 147–151.
54. For the requirements for admission see *El Mundo,* August 7, 1966, p. 5.
55. Late in 1967 the Labor Ministry issued a resolution regulating and facilitating attendance at universities of workers who are

qualified for such studies. Resolution No. 258 of November 29, 1967, established how workers could get relieved from production jobs, pointing out that priority would be given to workers who embarked on studies leading to careers most necessary for the economic and social development of the nation. Such workers were to receive subsidy payments. Havana Domestic Radio, November 29, 1967.

56. Reinaldo Casín González, "La Facultad Obrera y Campesina Julio A. Mella," *Cuba Socialista*, No. 47 (July, 1965), 85–92.
57. By 1968 enrollment at the Facultad Obrera of the University of Havana reached 8,368 students. "Daily News from the Cuban Radio" (USIA, Miami), December 12, 1968.
58. See Lee Lockwood's candid interview with Castro in *Playboy* (January, 1967), pp. 59–84.
59. See Mónica Sorín y Luis Gavilondo, "Acerca del rendimiento académico en una escuela universitaria," *Etnología y Folklore*, No. 2 (July–December, 1966), 75–92.
60. *Juventud Rebelde,* July 5, 1966, p. 2.
61. See for example Castro's December, 1966, University of Havana speech published among other places in *Vida Universitaria*, No. 197 (January, 1967), 3–16. For some of the party directives in the educational field see *Granma Weekly Review,* April 14, 1968, p. 8.
62. *Juventud Rebelde,* March 4, 1966, pp. 4–7. For another very interesting speech in which Crombet discusses youth and Communist society see *ibid.,* November 24, 1967, pp. 2–3.
63. *Ibid.* For an article discussing the "proper attitude" of UJC militants, published by the National UJC Committee, see *Juventud Rebelde,* April 23, 1968, p. 5.
64. The information on this incident was obtained by the author in the interview with Luis Fernández Berges, cited in note 35. Mr. Berges was a fifth year student and instructor at the University of Havana's Facultad of Technology. He was expelled from the University late in 1965 when he applied to leave Cuba.
65. *Ibid.* See also the series of articles by the associate editor of the *Sacramento Bee,* C. K. McClatchy, published in a pamphlet entitled *Cuba, 1965: A Reporter's Observations* (1965).
66. *Juventud Rebelde,* March 4, 1966, pp. 4–7.
67. See *Vida Universitaria,* No. 197 (January, 1967), 10.
68. This information has been obtained by the author in interviews with numerous students and teachers migrating from Cuba. Interviews with the following individuals proved extremely valuable: José Suárez, October 4, 1967; Luis Fernández Berges, October 19, 1967; Delfín González, October 13, 1967; Mirta González, October 14, 1967. In a speech on September 29, 1968, Castro himself deplored what he called "a wave of teenage delinquency and prostitution in Havana" and admitted that "teenagers have burned Cuban flags and torn down posters of Che Guevara." Havana Domestic Radio, September 29, 1968.

Bibliography

This study is based on published and unpublished materials as well as on interviews with students, student leaders, and participants in Cuba's political development. Interviews have been supplemented whenever possible with documentary evidence: newspapers, magazines, pamphlets, personal letters, tape recordings, speeches, and manifestos. Obviously, the interviews varied in value because of the intense involvement of some individuals and the faulty memories of others. All interviews were, therefore, used with caution. Cuba's weekly magazine *Bohemia* was of particular importance. Its section "En Cuba," which carried the events of the week, has been an invaluable source of information, as was *Diario de la Marina,* one of Cuba's oldest daily newspapers. *Diario de la Marina* was taken over by the Castro regime and ceased publication in 1960 while *Bohemia* continues to be published by the government. *Vida Universitaria,* a monthly magazine published by the University of Havana, is extremely important for both the pre-Castro and the revolutionary period. Three indispensable newspapers for anyone dealing with the revolution are the dailies *Juventud Rebelde,* official publication of the Union of Young Communists, *Noticias de Hoy* (commonly called *Hoy*), official publication of the Partido Socialista Popular, and *Revolución,* official publication of the 26th of July Movement. In 1966 the latter two merged to form *Granma,* the present official newspaper of Cuba's Communist Party. Since Havana's daily *El Mundo* ceased publication in 1969, *Granma* and *Juventud Rebelde* are the only two national dailies in Cuba. The monthly theoretical journal *Cuba Socialista,* published by the party, contains some very revealing articles. It ceased publication, however, in 1967 and its place has now been taken by *Pensamiento Crítico,* also published monthly. *OCLAE,* the official monthly publication of the Continental Organization of Latin American Students, contains some interesting articles on Latin American students, but its primary aim is to propagandize the views of the Cuban government among students and youth groups. Two journals, the quarterly *Revista de la Biblioteca Nacional José Martí*, and the bimonthly *Universidad de La Habana*, contain valuable historical articles. The bimonthly journal *Casa de las Américas* includes articles on the social sciences and literature by Cuban and Latin American writers. It is published by Casa de las Américas, a state cultural organization devoted to increasing contact among Cuban and Latin American intellectuals. The section on Cuba of the *Hispanic American Report*, a monthly review of events published by Stanford University from 1948 until 1964, served in many cases as a point of departure for further research. Although many books and periodical articles were consulted, only those relevant to this study have been included in the following bibliography.

I. BOOKS AND PAMPHLETS

Acuerdos de la Comisión Mixta de Reforma Universitaria. La Habana: Imprenta de la Universidad, 1959.

Baeza Flores, Alberto. *Las cadenas vienen de lejos*. México; Editorial Letras, 1960.

Batista, Fulgencio. *The Growth and Decline of the Cuban Republic*. New York: Devin Adair Co., 1964.

Bosch, Juan. *Cuba: La isla fascinante*. Santiago de Chile: Editorial Universitaria, S.A., 1955.

Boza, Luis. *La situación universitaria en Cuba*. Santiago de Chile: Editorial del Pacífico, S.A., 1962.

Bunn, Harriet and Gut, Ellen. *The Universities of Cuba, Haiti, and the Dominican Republic*. Washington, D.C.; Pan American Union, 1946.

Castellanos, Gerardo. *Panorama histórico: ensayo de cronología cubana*. La Habana: Ucar, García y Cía., 1934.

Casuso, Teresa. *Cuba and Castro*. New York: Random House, 1961.

Chapman, Charles E. *A History of the Cuban Republic*. New York: The MacMillan Co., 1927.

Chester, Edmund A. *A Sergeant Named Batista*. New York: Holt, 1954.

Commission on Cuban Affairs. *Problems of the New Cuba*. New York: Foreign Policy Association, 1935.

Conte Agüero, Luis. *Eduardo Chibás, el adalid de Cuba.* México: Editorial Jus, 1955.

Crítica y reforma universitarias. La Habana: Universidad de La Habana, 1959.

La cruz sigue en pie. Caracas: Directorio Revolucionario Estudiantil, n.d.

Cuarto Congreso Nacional Obrero de Unidad Sindical. *Resoluciones y acuerdos sobre la estructura orgánica de la CNOC.* La Habana, 1934.

Cuba 1967, the Educational Movement. Havana: Ministry of Education, 1967.

Del Consejo Universitario a la opinión pública. La Habana: Imprenta de la Universidad, 1953.

La destrucción de la enseñanza universitaria. Florida: Directorio Magisterial Cubano, n.d.

Doctrina del ABC: Manifiesto-Programa de 1932. La Habana: Editorial Cenit, 1942.

Draper, Theodore. *Castroism, Theory and Practice.* New York: Frederick A. Praeger, 1965.

Dubois, Jules. *Fidel Castro: Rebel-Liberator or Dictator?* Indianapolis: Bobbs-Merrill, 1959.

Dumpierre, Erasmo, *Mella, esbozo biográfico.* La Habana: Instituto de la Historia, 1965.

Emmerson, Donald K. *Students and Politics in Developing Nations.* New York: Frederick A. Praeger, 1968.

Fagen, Richard R. *Cuba: The Political Content of Adult Education.* Stanford: Stanford University, The Hoover Institution on War, Revolution, and Peace, 1964.

Fagg, John E. *Cuba, Haiti, and the Dominican Republic.* New Jersey: Prentice Hall Inc., 1965.

Figueroa y Miranda, Miguel. *Historia de la Agrupación Católica Universitaria.* La Habana, 1957.

Fitzgibbon, Russell H. *Cuba and the United States, 1900–1935.* Wisconsin: Menasha, 1935.

Foner, Philip S. *A History of Cuba in Its Relations with the United States.* 2 vols. New York: International Publishers, 1963.

Goldenberg, Boris. *The Cuban Revolution and Latin America.* New York: Frederick A. Praeger, 1965.

González Palacios, Carlos. *Revolución y seudo-revolución en Cuba.* La Habana, 1948.

Grupo Cubano de Investigaciones Económicas. *Un estudio sobre Cuba.* Coral Gables: University of Miami Press, 1963.

Guerra y Sánchez, Ramiro, et al. *Historia de la Nación Cubana.* 10 vols. La Habana: Editorial Historia de la Nación Cubana, S.A., 1952.

Guevara, Ernesto. *Man and Socialism in Cuba.* Havana: Book Institute, 1967.

Guggenheim, Harry F. *The United States and Cuba.* New York: The Macmillan Co., 1934.

Humboldt 7 y el comunismo cubano. Panamá: Directorio Revolucionario Estudiantil, n.d.

International Bank for Reconstruction and Development. *Report on Cuba.* Baltimore, 1951.

Julio A. Mella: documentos para su vida. Primer Congreso Nacional de Estudiantes. La Habana: Comisión Cubana de la UNESCO, 1964.

Kozolchyk, Boris. *The Political Biographies of Three Castro Officials.* Santa Monica: The Rand Corporation, 1966.

Krauss, Paul H. *Communist Policy in Cuba.* Columbia University: Unpublished M.A. Thesis, 1950.

Lamar Schweyer, Alberto. *Cómo cayó el presidente Machado.* Madrid: Espasa-Calpe, 1934.

Lazo, Mario. *Dagger in the Heart: American Policy Failures in Cuba.* New York: Funk & Wagnalls, 1968.

León, Rubén de. *El origen del mal.* Coral Gables: Service Offset Printers, 1964.

LeRoy y Gálvez. *La Universidad de La Habana: síntesis histórica.* La Habana: Imprenta de la Universidad, 1960.

Lipset, Seymour Martin, ed. *Student Politics.* New York: Basic Books, Inc., 1967.

Lockwood, Lee. *Castro's Cuba, Cuba's Fidel.* New York: The Macmillan Co., 1967.

La lucha revolucionaria contra el imperialismo. La Habana: Editora Popular de Cuba y del Caribe, 1960.

MacGaffey, Wyatt and Barnett, Clifford R. *Twentieth Century Cuba: The Background of the Castro Revolution.* New York: Doubleday and Co., 1965.

Martínez Villena, Rubén. *La pupila insomne.* La Habana: Editorial Lex, n.d.

Matthews, Herbert. *The Cuban Story.* New York: George Braziller, 1961.

Mella, Julio Antonio. *Ensayos revolucionarios.* La Habana: Editora Popular de Cuba y del Caribe, 1960.

Merle, Robert. *Moncada: Premier combat de Fidel Castro.* Paris: Robert Laffont, 1965.

Nelson, Lowry. *Rural Cuba.* Minneapolis: University of Minnesota Press, 1950.

El partido comunista y los problemas de la revolución en Cuba. La Habana: Comité Central del Partido Comunista de Cuba, 1933.

Pflaum, Irving P. *Tragic Island: How Communism Came to Cuba.* New Jersey: Prentice Hall, 1961.

Portell Vilá, Herminio. *Historia de Cuba en sus relaciones con los Estados Unidos y España.* 4 vols. La Habana: Editorial Jesús Montero, 1930.

Portuondo de Castro, Juan M. *Cómo se apoderaron los comunistas de la Universidad de La Habana.* Florida: Directorio Magistrial Cubano, 1962.

Püig y Pupo, José R. R. *Apuntes sobre la escuela de Derecho y la Universidad de La Habana.* La Habana: Imprenta de la Universidad, 1959.

Quesada, Gonzalo de, ed. *Obras completas de Martí.* 79 vols. La Habana: Editorial Trópico, 1937.

La reforma de la enseñanza superior en Cuba. Cuba: Consejo Superior de Universidades, 1962.

Riera Hernández, Mario. *Historial Obrero Cubano.* Miami: Rema Press, 1965.

Roa, Raúl. *En pie.* Santa Clara: Universidad Central de Las Villas, 1959.

Roa, Raúl. *Quince años después.* La Habana: Selecta, 1950.

Roa, Raúl. *Retorno a la alborada.* 2 vols. Las Villas: Universidad de Las Villas, 1964.

Roca, Blas (Francisco Calderío). *Las experiencias de Cuba.* La Habana: Editorial Páginas, 1939.

Roca, Blas (Francisco Calderío). *The Cuban Revolution.* New York: New Century Publications, 1961.

Rodríguez Morejón, Gerardo. *Fidel Castro: Biografía.* La Habana: P. Fernández y Cía., 1959.

Ruiz, Ramón Eduardo. *Cuba: The Making of a Revolution.* Amherst: The University of Massachusetts Press, 1968.

Seers, Dudley, ed. *Cuba: The Economic and Social Revolution.* Chapel Hill: The University of North Carolina Press, 1964.

Selser, Gregorio, ed. *La revolución cubana.* Buenos Aires: Editorial Palestra, 1960.

La sierra y el llano. La Habana: Casa de las Américas, 1961.

Smith, Robert F., ed. *Background to Revolution: The Development of Modern Cuba.* New York: Alfred A. Knopf, 1966.

Smith, Robert F., ed. *The United States and Cuba: Business and*

Diplomacy, 1917–1960. New York: Bookman Associates, 1961.

Spencer, David, ed. *Student Politics in Latin America.* United States National Student Association, 1965.

Suárez, Andrés. *Cuba: Castroism and Communism, 1959–1966.* Cambridge: M.I.T. Press, 1967.

Suárez Rivas, Eduardo. *Un pueblo crucificado.* Coral Gables: Service Offset Printers, 1964.

Taber, Robert. *M–26: Biography of a Revolution.* New York: Lyle Stuart, 1961.

Torriente Brau, Pablo. *La última sonrisa de Trejo.* La Habana: Delegación del gobierno en el Capitolio Nacional, 1959.

Trece documentos de la insurrección. La Habana: Organización nacional de bibliotecas ambulantes y populares, 1959.

U.S. Congress, House, *Annual Reports of the War Department: Report of Enrique José Varona,* 50th Cong., 2nd sess., 1901, vol. I.

U.S. Congress, Senate, Committee on the Judiciary, *Communist Threat to the U.S. Through the Caribbean, Hearings.* 86th Cong., 2nd sess., part 10, 1960.

U.S. Office of Education, *Educational Data: Cuba,* Washington, D.C.: Government Printing Office, November, 1962.

La Universidad de La Habana al Consejo Ejecutivo y a la Asamblea General de la Unión de Universidades de América Latina. La Habana: Universidad de La Habana, 1964.

Welles, Sumner. *Relations Between the U.S. and Cuba.* State Department, Latin American Series, no 7. Washington, D.C.: Government Printing Office, 1934.

Weyl, Nathaniel. *Red Star Over Cuba.* New York: Hillman McFadden, 1961.

Wood, Bryce. *The Making of the Good Neighbor Policy.* New York: W. W. Morton & Co., 1967.

Worcester, Donald E. and Schaeffer, Wendell G. *The Growth and Culture of Latin America.* New York: Oxford University Press, 1956.

II. ARTICLES

Agüayo, Alfredo M. "Factores cualitativos de nuestra decadencia escolar." *Revista Bimestre Cubana* (March-April, 1926).

Agüayo, Alfredo M. "La Universidad en la postguerra." *Revista de La Habana* No. 17 (January, 1944).

Aja, Pedro Vicente. "La crisis de la Universidad de La Habana." *Ensayos.* Quito (August, 1962).

Bailey, Norman A. "The U.S. as Caudillo." *Journal of Inter-American Studies* (July, 1963).

Bustamante y Montoro, A. S. "Situación del pensamiento filosófico actual." *Escuela y revolución en Cuba,* No. 3 (January-February, 1964).

Cabrera, Luis Rolando. "La formación de profesionales en las universidades cubanas." *El Siglo Veinte* (Mexico), No. 64 (March, 1966).

Carvajal, Ladislao G. "Sin libros no hay conciencia, no hay comunismo." *Cuba Socialista* (March, 1964).

Casín González, Reinaldo. "La Facultad Obrera y Campesina Julio A. Mella." *Cuba Socialista* (July, 1965).

Chibás, Eddy. "Hacia dónde va Cuba." *Bohemia* (August 26, 1934).

Cronon, E. David. "Interpreting the New Good Neighbor Policy: The Cuban Crisis of 1933." *The Hispanic American Historical Review* 39 (November, 1959).

Cueto, Mario G. del. "Unión Insurreccional Revolucionaria." *Bohemia* (June 15, 1947).

Fagen, Richard R. "Mass Moblization in Cuba: The Symbolism of Struggle." *Journal of International Affairs,* No. 20 (1966).

Fagen, Richard R. "The Cuban Revolution: Enemies and Friends." In David J. Finlay et al. *Enemies in Politics.* Chicago: Rand McNally & Co., 1967.

García Buchaca, Edith. "Las transformaciones culturales de la revolución cubana." *Cuba Socialista* (January, 1964).

García Gallo, Jorge G. "Julio Antonio Mella y la fundación del Partido Comunista." *Universidad de La Habana,* No. 174 (July-August, 1965).

Gil, Federico. "Antecedents of the Cuban Revolution." *The Centennial Review of Arts and Sciences* (Summer, 1962).

Grau San Martín, Ramón. "El nacionalismo Auténtico y sus leyes." *Bohemia* (August 26, 1934).

Grau San Martín, Ramón. "The Cuban Terror." *The Nation* 140 (April 3, 1935).

Grobart, Fabio. "El movimiento obrero cubano de 1925 a 1933." *Cuba Socialista* (August, 1966).

Habel, Janette, "Le Procés de Marcos Rodríguez et les probèmes de l'unité du Mouvement Revolutionnaire à Cuba." *Les Temps Modernes,* No. 219–220 (September, 1964).

Hart, Armando. "La enseñanza técnica y profesional de nivel medio y universitario." *Cuba Socialista* (February, 1966).

Hart, Armando. "La trascendencia del IV CLAE para el movimiento estudiantil y antiimperialista de nuestro continente." *Cuba Socialista* (September, 1966).

Hart, Armando. "Objetivos de la educación secundaria en Cuba." *Boletín de la Universidad de Chile* (June, 1965).

Hartman, Heinz. "Sociology in Cuba." *American Sociological Review* 28 (August, 1963).

Hennessy, C. A. M. "The Roots of Cuban Nationalism." *International Affairs* (London) 39 (July, 1963).

Irisarri, José M. "Cómo nació y cómo murió la Comisión Ejecutiva." *Bohemia* (August 26, 1934).

Lavín, Pablo F. "El estado cubano y sus problemas educacionales." *Universidad de La Habana* 24 (July-December, 1947).

LeRoy y Gálvez, Luis Felipe. "El Plan de Estudios de 1863 en la Universidad de La Habana." *Universidad de La Habana* (March-June, 1964).

LeRoy, y Gálvez, Luis Felipe. "La Universidad de La Habana en su etapa republicana." *Revista de la Biblioteca Nacional José Martí* (April-June, 1966).

Maldonado-Denis, Manuel. "The Situation of Cuba's Intellectuals." *The Christian Century* 85 (January 17, 1968).

Mañach, Jorge. "Revolution in Cuba." *Foreign Affairs* 12 (October, 1933).

Marinello, Juan. "Universidad y cultura." *Universidad de La Habana,* No. 159 (January-February, 1963).

Mencía Cobas, Mario. "Por qué luchan los estudiantes en América latina?" *Universidad de La Habana,* No. 181 (September-October, 1966).

Moré Benítez, J. B. "La revolución técnica y la Escuela Universitaria de Ciencias Políticas." *Cuba Socialista* (September, 1964).

Mortillado, Gaspar. "Presencia de Tina Modotti en la vida de Julio A. Mella." *Universidad de La Habana,* No. 174 (July-August, 1965).

Pérez Humberto and Luz, Félix de la. "Contribución a un diálogo." *Teoría y Práctica,* No. 31 (October, 1966).

Portuondo, José A. "Los intelectuales y la Revolución." *Cuba Socialista* (June, 1964).

Quintana, Jorge. "La muerte de Antonio Guiteras." *Bohemia* (September 15, 22, 1946).

Rivero, Adolfo. "La Unión de Jóvenes Comunistas de Cuba." *Cuba Socialista* (August, 1962).

Rodríguez, Carlos Rafael. "La Reforma Universitaria." *Cuba Socialista* (February, 1962).

Rodríquez, Carlos Rafael. "Vigencia de Julio A. Mella." *Universidad de La Habana,* No. 174 (July-August, 1965).

Roig de Luechsenring, Emilio. "La lucha cubana contra la Enmienda Platt, la intervención y el imperalismo." *Universidad de La Habana,* No. 13 (June-July, 1937).

Roucek, Joseph S. "Pro-Communist Revolution in Cuban Education." *Journal of Inter-American Studies* 6 (July, 1964).

Serviat, Pedro. "Mella, la clase obrera y los intelectuales." *Universidad de La Habana,* No. 179 (May-June, 1966).

Sorín, Mónica y Gavilondo, Luis. "Acerca del rendimiento académico en una escuela universitaria." *Etnología y Folklore* 2 (July-December, 1966).

Stokes, William S. "National and Local Violence in Cuban Politics." *Southwestern Social Science Q* 34 (September, 1963).

Stokes, Williams S. "The Cuban Revolution and the Presidential Elections of 1948." *Hispanic American Historical Review* 37 (February, 1951).

Thomas, Hugh. "Middle Class Politics and the Cuban Revolution." In Claudio Véliz, ed. *The Politics of Conformity in Latin America.* London: Oxford University Press, 1967.

Thomson, Charles A. "The Cuban Revolution: Fall of Machado." *Foreign Policy Reports* 11 (December 18, 1935).

Thomson, Charles A. "The Cuban Revolution: Reform and Reaction." *Foreign Policy Reports* 11 (January 1, 1936).

Torriente Brau, Pablo. "La nueva actitud universitaria." *Bohemia* (January 14, 1934).

Torroella, Gustavo. "Ideals and Values of Young People in Cuba." *International Journal of Adult and Youth Education* 16 (1964).

Vignier, Marta. "La Universidad de La Habana." *Siglo Veinte* (Mexico), No. 63 (February, 1966).

Index

ABC, 29, 30, 32, 38, 39, 44; influence on the students, 29, 30, 32
Acción Revolucionaria Guiteras (ARG), 49, 50
Agrupación Católica Universitaria, 95
Ala Izquierda Estudiantil, 27–28
Alarcón, Ricardo, 90, 93, 161n
Alonso, Aurelio, 119
Anti-Clerical Federation, 21
Anti-Imperialist League, 21, 28, 38
April 9 Plan, 99–100
Arce, José, 20
Army, 17, 27, 32, 34–35, 38–39, 40, 41, 44, 45, 58, 61, 62, 70, 88, 106, 138n; see also Revolutionary Armed Forces
Artime, Manuel, 96, 104, 157–158n
Association of Young Rebels (AJR), 101
auténticos, see Partido Revolucionario Cubano
Baliño, Carlos, 21
Batista, Fulgencio, 35, 36, 39, 40, 41, 43, 44, 45, 50, 56, 87, 89, 99; alliance with the Directorio Estudiantil Universitario, 34, 36; and Grau's overthrow, 39, 40; as arbiter of Cuba's politics, 45–46; constitutional presidency, 46–48; coup d'état of

1952, 56, 57, 58; FEU opposition to, 58–70; Directorio Revolucionario opposition to, 70–86; and the Communists, 47, 83
Bay of Pigs, 99, 100
Blanco Rico, Antonio, 73
"bogotazo," 53–54
Boitel, Pedro L., 89, 90, 154n
bonches, 51; see student violence
Caffrey, Jefferson, 40
caimán barbudo, El, 118
Caracas pact, 86, 153n
Carbó Servia, Juan Pedro, 73, 80, 81, 83
Cárdenas, Lázaro, 45
carta de México, La, 73
Castro, Fidel, 61, 62, 70, 85; as a university student, 52–54; and the Cayo Confites expedition, 52; and the "bogotazo," 53–54, 148n; and the Moncada attack, 62–63; and expedition from Mexico, 73, 74; and the Directorio Revolucionario, 73, 74, 81–82, 84, 86, 88–89; and the Communists, 82, 85, 101–103, 152n, 157n; and the Junta de Liberación Cubana, 84–85; and the Caracas pact, 86; and the FEU, 89–91; and University autonomy, 91–93, 111–112; and student opposition, 94–100, 130–135; and the Directorio